D1638980

80 Creative Prayer Ideas

Published by
The Bible Reading Fellowship
15 The Chambers, Vineyard
Abingdon OX14 3FE
United Kingdom
Tel: +44 (0)1865 319700
Email: enquiries@brf.org.uk
Website: www.brf.org.uk
BRF is a Registered Charity

ISBN 978 1 84101 688 7
First published 2014
10 9 8 7 6 5 4 3 2 1 0
All rights reserved

Acknowledgments
Unless otherwise stated, scripture quotations are taken from the Holy Bible, New International Version (Anglicised edition), copyright © 1979, 1984, 2011 by Biblica. Used by permission of Hodder & Stoughton Publishers, an Hachette UK company. All rights reserved. 'NIV' is a registered trademark of Biblica. UK trademark number 1448790.

Scripture quotations from the Holy Bible, Today's New International Version, copyright © 2004 by Biblica. Used by permission of Hodder & Stoughton Publishers, an Hachette UK company. All rights reserved. 'TNIV' is a registered trademark of Biblica.

Scripture quotations marked (NLT) are taken from the Holy Bible, New Living Translation, copyright © 1996, 2004. Used by permission of Tyndale House Publishers, Inc., Wheaton, Illinois 60189. All rights reserved.

Cover photos: Background: Hemera/Thinkstock; Candles: Istockphoto/Thinkstock

A catalogue record for this book is available from the British Library

Printed by Gutenberg Press, Tarxien, Malta

80 Creative Prayer Ideas

Prayer

Ideas

A resource for church and group use

Claire Daniel

For my Grandpa, Walter Hooley. You are wise beyond your 94 years.
Your stories and strength inspire me simply to trust God,
whom you have served so faithfully.

Acknowledgements

Naomi Starkey and all involved at BRF, my gratitude to you for the faith you have shown in me and my ideas. Your God-given vision, support and grace have enabled me to develop as we have shared this journey.

Not only does it take a whole community to raise a child, but I have learnt that the same is very much true of a book—particularly when doing both at once, for the first time! Thank you to each and every person who made this book possible. Every friend or family member who has offered a word, a smile, a hug, prayers or offered practical help—you have made a difference, both in the development of my writing and in my faith journey so far.

My parents, your love and practical support have been invaluable all my life and such a significant constant in my recent journey into parenthood and publication.

Chris and Graham, your unconditional love and prayers mean so much to me. Thank you for the writing haven of your Green Room, tea on tap and grandparent time for Ewan.

To the other Claire for your prayers, encouraging words and for all the hugs, laughter and lemon and lime. I am blessed that we share life, faith and taking on the world together.

Rachel Turner, thank you for answering all my questions with great enthusiasm and for welcoming me into the BRF family with such grace and kindness.

Special thanks to my housegroup and my lovely 'Essex girls', who experienced my creative prayer ideas in their infancy and encouraged me to take them further. I hope you like what those prayers have grown up to be. Thanks to Oli Nicholls for inspiring me to persevere and keep pushing doors.

Thank you to Sue Coyne and Naomi Gill for your presentation advice and support, getting my ideas polished, ready to place them in BRFs care.

My boys, Gary and Ewan. The life I share with the one who rests his tiny head on my shoulder and the one who lets me rest on his is one of my greatest joys. I couldn't have written this book without your love and support and the strength and grace God gives me daily.

Preface

Creative prayer has long been a feature of my journey with God—an integral part of some of the most significant and memorable moments in the development of my faith so far. There have been numerous times, at intervals, when I have personally spent time in prayer, alone or as part of a group or congregational worship, using simple, active prayer responses. These have been experiences of important reflection, sometimes painful or cathartic but mainly joyful, reassuring and uplifting.

Moments spent in creative reflection give precious time over to listening to God in prayer, as well as offering worship or requests to him. Creative prayer activities also help at those times when our prayers are difficult to form into words or when we feel we lack eloquence. As a form of worship, response and communication, creative prayer enables many Christians to discover a level of closeness and connection with God quite different from the other types of prayer that form their 'usual' worship experience.

The written prayers, doodles, objects and Bible verses that I have kept from times spent in creative prayer remain some of the most treasured memories and keepsakes of my faith. They serve as a reminder both of the things I shared with God and the things he communicated to me, a wonderful sign of all that God has done for me and the journey that I have walked with him so far. They also act as visual reminders to continue to pray for certain things, and to keep on persevering, growing and developing in my faith.

In writing this book, my aim is to make creative methods of prayer accessible to everyone and anyone who wants to engage with God in an imaginative, alternative way. The book has been put together in a user-friendly format, designed to be used or adapted to suit a variety of group, church or individual needs and settings. Some of these ideas may be familiar, as they are, to a degree, adaptations of widely known ways of bringing prayers creatively to God. However, the majority have occurred to me during my own moments of reflection, when I have not been consciously trying to devise a specific idea.

I pray that this book may be a helpful resource to you, whenever and wherever you choose to use it. May you, and all those with whom you share these ideas, find great joy, rest and renewal as you explore the ways to meet with God that best suit you.

Prayer is everywhere. Prayer is language used to respond to the most that has been said to us, with the potential for saying all that is in us.
EUGENE PETERSON, *HOPE: A POCKET INSPIRATIONS BOOK* (SUMMERSIDE PRESS), P. 58

Contents

Our personal walk with God

Foreword

This is a book that is so needed in our word-filled world! It is wonderfully creative, helping us to engage with all of our being in the whole business of listening to, walking with, waiting for and talking with God. It provides biblically based ideas to make prayer accessible to an individual, small group or church congregation in ways that are engaging, stimulating and fun.

So many of us find it hard getting down to prayer, whether we try on our own or with others in a small group or in a church setting. Often this is because we rely solely on using verbal tools to 'pray'. Although that does work for some of us, others need to engage more actively in the 'doing' and so become able to connect with the Bible passage, themes or issues in more interactive ways which enable prayer to flow for themselves and for others.

I hope this book will spur on leaders who want to include creative praying in church services and home groups as well as individuals who want to explore new ways of encountering God in the place of prayer. Jesus clearly showed us our responsibilities as his followers: to pray for his kingdom to come and for his will to be done in and for our families and our neighbours, in our communities, our nation and our world. Let's use these creative methods of prayer and see where God leads us as we sense our own prayer journey developing, reaching up to God and out to those he puts on our heart to pray for and about.

Jane Holloway, World Prayer Centre, Birmingham

Introduction

The term 'creative prayer' often evokes very mixed and strong reactions. For some Christians, it generates an enthusiasm to pray in new or inventive ways and be guided into a physical, active response to God. A desire to worship God in this way almost literally 'bubbles up' in certain personality types, who are naturally eager to use a variety of props or reflective methods in order to communicate with God. In other Christians, however fervent their desire to bring their prayers to God, the term produces a sinking sense of dread or even abject fear. The mere mention of it is swiftly met with cries of 'I'm not creative!'

If you have used creative prayer methods countless times already, you may wish to skip to the chapters containing themed prayer ideas and use them to start your own ideas flowing straight away. However, you may still find it helpful to take time to read the rest of this introduction, designed as a guide to using creative prayer, as it contains some general ideas for prayer and reflection that can be adapted to fit various settings, themes and occasions.

Many Christians also find that the style of creative prayer is a great leap from the more traditional, liturgical approach with which they are familiar. There are also a great many Christians, actively involved in ministry and familiar with creative prayer, whose desire to use it with their groups or congregations is overwhelmed by the regular demands of their everyday family or work circumstances. Involvement in existing church commitments and paid or voluntary service to God, as well as the pace of life in general, can make the practicalities of organising a creative prayer event an unbearable added pressure for even the most energetic of us. This book sets out to be equally relevant and user-friendly for those to whom creative prayer is a new prospect as for those who are entirely familiar and even 'expert' at it. I pray that, whatever your current need or viewpoint may be, you might keep the book handy for those times when you need a ready-to-use idea or collection of ideas for a particular theme. It may even inspire you to begin your own journey of using creative methods and discovering new ways to pray.

Setting up creative prayer stations, preparing resources and sourcing ideas can be very time-consuming, whether or not you feel you have a flair for it and despite (or perhaps due to) the enormous number of online resources available. The prayer ideas in this book are deliberately designed to provide a complete tool-kit, with guidance on everything you need, to take the stress out of organising creative prayer.

The rest of this introduction provides support with the practical side of planning and implementing creative prayer, as well as some 'general' creative prayer ideas that can be used as individual activities or added to the ones included in the subsequent themed chapters. For example, if you wanted to set up a prayer event with five, six or more stations rather than four, the 'general ideas' section will enable you to mix and match, add your own ideas and adapt them to your requirements.

Setting up

There are various practical aspects involved in organising a creative prayer activity. The practicalities will vary enormously, depending on whether you are preparing a single activity for a group or congregation, using the prayer ideas at home with your family or holding a creative prayer event or workshop with a number of stations available. You will need to take into consideration the venue you are using and the space available. If you are going to set up a series of stations, you will need, of course, to think more carefully about setting up the space than if you are using a single prayer idea in a small group or church setting.

If you are preparing a complete creative prayer event with four to six or even more stations for people to circulate around in their own time, you will need to put in some groundwork. Ensuring that all is ready in the room itself, in addition to preparing each station and its content, is important. This may be relatively easy in some churches, halls, homes or school settings but may require a little more adjustment and assistance in others. You should think about the changes you may need to make to the overall room and its appearance, which might include some of the following considerations.

Furniture

Make sure you have enough chairs, tables, cushions or beanbags and that carpets and flooring are clean and suitable for use. Set up tables with chairs ready, if needed. Consider whether you will need tablecloths or other decorations to fit with the overall theme, and anything else that will help to provide a calm, relaxed atmosphere in which to focus on prayer.

Lighting and sound

The right kind of lighting is crucial to create the appropriate atmosphere, but your choices will depend on what type of stations you choose to set up. Some may work best if dimly lit, using small lights or candles, but any involving writing, reading or drawing may need some extra lighting. Be creative! Use the lighting options available and bring along extra lamps as required, such as small desk lamps or decorative table lamps.

If some of the stations include the use of music, think about what would work best—a CD player or some kind of MP3 device and appropriate headphones. You may want to engage musicians in your church or group, or use a recording, to have quiet music playing for the duration of the activity. This is not always necessary, of course, but it can aid reflection and help people focus; there are also times when silence during a time of prayer is more appropriate. Playing recorded worship music as part of a creative prayer event or service does not require a specific licence, as it is classed as part of an 'act of worship'. However, if you wish to clarify anything regarding the use of music in your chosen venue, information can be found on the Christian Copyright Licensing International website at www.ccli.co.uk.

Power sources

Do ensure that you have adequate power sockets near any stations that require them (for example, if you are using a small lamp or fan). Checking these before you set up will prevent you from having to move stations around at the last minute.

Health and safety

There will inevitably be some basic health and safety considerations in arranging even the simplest creative prayer stations. Most of them will be common-sense issues regarding safe use of power sockets, managing water spillages and furniture lifting. Make sure that you and all those attending are aware of the location of fire exits, extinguishers, toilets and any other amenities specific to the venue, particularly if it is not normally used as a multipurpose space. You may need to return chairs and other furniture to their previous layouts, for other sessions or services. Also, do check that the whole space used is generally clean and tidy.

Make sure you have sufficient fire safety equipment and knowledge specific to your chosen venue, before as well as during your prayer event, and check that you meet fire regulations regarding access if you are changing the furniture layout. You may also need to check the situation regarding the use of naked flames or cooking, if you plan to make these part of any of the stations, to avoid any hazards and to ensure that you don't accidentally set off smoke alarms.

Handwashing facilities

Many creative prayer ideas, by their very nature, will involve a certain degree of mess, and any stations that involve paint, water or sand may need to be supplied with items such as paper towels or hand wipes. You might even set up the stations near a sink or toilet to facilitiate handwashing. It may be necessary to keep a watch on the messier stations during an event and 'reset' them periodically or clear up spills. You will also need to provide handwashing facilities if you are using sticky materials, such as bread dough, modelling clay or glue sticks, or if people need to prepare for any food-based creative prayers.

Kitchen requirements

If you are planning to provide a station involving food (including baking or pre-prepared salt dough or biscuits, for example), you should check that there are kitchen facilities available and equipped for your needs. If you choose to bake bread or biscuits as part of the prayer activity, food hygiene and kitchen safety should also be factored in, particularly if younger children are involved.

Replenishing stations

Most of the prayer ideas will require the replenishment of resources, or a large quantity of them to begin with, especially if you are using a single activity as a group or congregation or if you are anticipating a large number of people. As the event proceeds, it is probably a good idea to have someone assigned to keeping the stations tidy and 'reset' at intervals. It is important (though probably quite obvious) that the stations are presented in a user-friendly way and kept tidy, in order to be experienced fully by each person.

Some of the prayer ideas include the use of bowls or trays of water, or the use of ice cubes. In addition to handwashing facilities, you may also need to consider how you will fill, refill or manage water use. You will probably want to use plastic tablecloths or sheets to protect tables and carpets from the inevitable spills.

Props and useful kit

Each prayer idea in this book includes a guide to the items that will be needed. The two templates on pages 188 and 189, for the spinner and pinwheel, may be photocopied from this book or downloaded from www.brfonline.org.uk/9781841016887/.

There are also some generally useful props or 'kit' that you may want to use, in addition to those detailed for each individual prayer idea. If you are not already well stocked with these ministry 'essentials', you will probably start to stockpile supplies, which in turn can generate new prayer ideas. Here is a list, which is far from exhaustive.

- Plastic sheets or tablecloths (either 'standard' ones or camping-style groundsheets).

- Tables and chairs. Size and quantity required will depend on your venue, expected attendance and the prayer stations you are planning.

- Soft furnishings, such as cushions, beanbags, small sofas or blankets. Also think of items that will be useful for enhancing stations, such as small desk or table lamps or even some decorative mats or covers in appropriate colours, to match a theme.

- Craft resources. The possibilities are endless, but a basic craft kit would include glue sticks, scissors, paper, coloured card, sparkly wrapping paper, ribbons, pipe cleaners, felt-tip pens, sticky tape, sticky notes, adhesive tack, paint, paint pots, brushes, sponges, balloons, tissue paper, sequins, buttons, rolls of paper and large sheets of card or fabric (for example, voile or bed sheets).

- Bowls, trays and food equipment. If your prayer activity involves anything food-based, you will need to provide suitable serving bowls, trays or plates. If you are using paint, modelling dough or other messy craft items, you should find a suitable receptacle for the activity, enabling several hands or feet to dip into them, one or more at a time. If you are using dough (either modelling dough or bread or biscuit dough), you will need to make some simple tools available, such as plastic cutlery, rolling pins or wooden cocktail sticks, to shape, manipulate and decorate items.

Internet

The internet can be an excellent source of images, photos, music and outlined shapes or templates for prayer activities. Although this book is intended to reduce the time taken in searching online for prayer ideas, some of the activities require you to draw or print shapes or templates to use, which can be found online or in a computer wordprocessing package. There are, of course, many prayer ideas available online that you can access to supplement those included here, should you wish to.

Bibles and books

Some of the prayer ideas include a Bible or printed scripture in the 'What I need' list, although I have also assumed that some stories will be familiar to users. Depending on your audience, you may feel it necessary or helpful to include a Bible or printed version of a certain story—for example, the story of Zacchaeus.

A selection of Bible versions, plus other inspirational books, leaflets or tracts, can provide a great resource for prayer activities related to a specific verse of scripture. They are also useful if you want to set up a station that is a less structured space, browsing and reading from a selection of material and reflecting or praying unguided. These materials could include Bible verse cards, inspiring quotes, stories and poems.

Getting started

Each prayer idea is set out to give you all the information and instruction needed to resource and plan each activity. You may wish just to use the idea and create your own prayer card or instruction sheet for your station. Alternatively, you can write or type out the wording for the prayers as suggested in the book for each station. You may want to use the 'Reflect' and 'Pray' parts, and possibly the 'Prayer focus:' and 'Bible reflection', as appropriate for your specific audience.

General prayer ideas

The following ideas are useful for creating additional stations if you want to provide a larger creative prayer event. They can be used as a single activity for a group or even congregation to use, and can be adapted to fit with various themes.

- Sticky note prayers: sticky notes are readily available in various shops and can be found in a variety of colours, sizes and shapes (for example, heart- or star-shaped).

- Graffiti prayer wall: use a large roll or piece of paper or card as a space for people to add individual prayers, drawings or Bible verses on a theme, creating a collective wall of prayer graffiti. You can make the wall more structured by preparing uniform shapes for each person to write in, or it can be done 'freestyle'.

- Whiteboard or chalk prayers: this is ideal for any prayers to which people will respond by 'wiping away'. This approach is good for forgiveness or 'fresh start' prayers. Regular or jumbo chalks can be used on either boards or pavements and wiped away with a damp cloth.

- Bubble prayers: individual bubble pots, a shared bubble mixture tray or a bubble machine can be used in a variety of prayer activities or illustrations.

- Shredder prayers: using a paper shredder is a rather noisy but very powerful method of 'letting go' or giving things to God, in response to prayers for forgiveness and moving forward with God.

- Flash paper: this special paper appears to burn when lit, then vanishes without a trace. You can write a word or prayer on it— for example, 'sin'—making an excellent gospel illustration or prayer activity. Adult supervision is required if using flash paper with a younger age group.

- 'Pick a promise' box: a traditional prayer tool, this is available to buy ready-made or you can create your own mini prayer box. It contains tiny rolled-up scrolls, printed with biblical promises. The scrolls usually stand upright in a 'honeycomb' formation but can be stacked inside or tied with pieces of ribbon. The box could be a gift to take away and treasure or a prayer station focus, with scrolls to be read and replaced after each use.

- Tactile prayer objects: examples might be small wooden prayer crosses or hearts, or pebbles from a beach or riverbed. Holding a tactile object during prayer helps to focus the mind and can also inspire prayers.

- Prayer pebbles: casting pebbles into water is a powerful and well-known method of creative response to God. It can be used in a variety of situations and represents a physical act of giving something up to God or symbolising God's cleansing power.

- Modelling clay prayers: modelling clay or dough can be bought or made in a variety of colours and is adaptable to suit a variety of themed prayer activities, including those related to 'moulding' and 'transformation'.

Section 1

Walking with the Bible

Chapter 1

Men of faith

Daniel: courage in the face of adversity

Prayer focus: Using the story of Daniel's courage, to bring before God the 'lions' in our lives, asking for his help to face difficulty and giving thanks for the times when he has provided the strength needed to overcome adversity.

 Bible reflection: *When he came near the den, he called to Daniel in an anguished voice, 'Daniel, servant of the living God, has your God, whom you serve continually, been able to rescue you from the lions?' Daniel answered, 'May the king live forever! My God sent his angel, and he shut the mouths of the lions. They have not hurt me, because I was found innocent in his sight.'*
DANIEL 6:20–22

What I need

- Large picture or photo of a lion, open-mouthed (hand-drawn, if you feel very competent, or printed at A4 or larger)
- Paper or card 'mouth' to fit over the mouth in the picture, able to open and close
- Triangular paper or cardboard 'teeth' (pre-cut shapes or triangular sticky notes)
- Adhesive tack (if not using sticky notes)
- Pens or pencils

- Sticky tape or glue
- Copies of Bible, storybook or printed version of the story of Daniel in the lions' den

Set up the image of the lion on a large flipchart, pinboard or table, as required. Make sure the 'mouth' is stuck on, hinged with glue or sticky tape, and that it opens and closes easily.

Reflect: Reflect on the Bible story of Daniel and his trust in God, even in extreme adversity. Consider your own need for strength to face those circumstances or emotions that seem like sharp-toothed lions in your life. These may include seemingly insurmountable worries, difficult relationships or personal struggles in your own experience or that of people known to you.

Pray: Bring these 'lions' before God, trusting that he is a powerful God who gives us the strength to overcome. Take a paper or cardboard tooth and write on it a word or prayer about your worries. Have faith that God can help you overcome your 'lions'.

Take some time, holding the tooth, to pray about these circumstances, fears and impossible situations, giving them into God's care. Give thanks, also, for times when he has helped you overcome the 'impossible' in the past.

When you are ready, lift the mouth of the lion open and stick your 'tooth' of fears or worries on to the space inside. Pray as you do this, remembering that God's strength helps us overcome our 'lions' too.

In a final response, firmly shut the lion's mouth over the sharp, worrisome 'teeth'. Leave these things with God, and rejoice as you look at the lion's mouth, now tightly shut.

David: repentance and renewal

Prayer focus: Using Psalm 32, to reflect on God's power to transform our hearts and offer forgiveness and renewal when we seek his grace.

 Bible reflection: *Rejoice in the Lord and be glad, you righteous; sing, all you who are upright in heart!*
PSALM 32:11

What I need

• Bible or printed copies of Psalm 32

• Smaller cards printed with verse 1, 5, 7 or 11 (several copies of each)

Reflect: Read the whole of Psalm 32, or the selected verses below, reflecting on the words before you begin to pray.

Blessed is the one whose transgressions are forgiven, whose sins are covered. (Verse 1)

Then I acknowledged my sin to you and did not cover up my iniquity. I said, 'I will confess my transgressions to the Lord.' And you forgave the guilt of my sin. (Verse 5)

You are my hiding-place; you will protect me from trouble and surround me with songs of deliverance. (Verse 7)

Rejoice in the Lord and be glad, you righteous; sing, all you who are upright in heart! (Verse 11)

Pray: Thank God for the sins he has forgiven and use the verses above to help you confess the wrongs you need to bring before God. Know that he holds out the offer of forgiveness, even before we repent. Know that you are blessed.

Pray your own 'song of deliverance', giving thanks to God for his protection in times of trouble and the grace that sets us free. Pray a prayer of rejoicing, knowing that God hears your prayers and offers forgiveness.

Take a small verse card away with you, as a reminder that God forgives those who truly repent and that he wants you to live in freedom.

Zacchaeus: prayer of restoration

Prayer focus: To bring to God those areas of our life where our faith or ability feels 'small', asking God to use our 'little' to do 'big' things for his kingdom. To pray for restoration and a chance to serve him as Zacchaeus did.

 Bible reflection: *Jesus said to him, 'Today salvation has come to this house, because this man, too, is a son of Abraham. For the Son of Man came to seek and to save the lost.'*
LUKE 19:9–10

What I need

- Small blank people shapes (pre-cut from plain card or paper)

- Large tree drawn or printed on to paper or card (large enough to hold a number of the cut-out people shapes)

- Sticky tack

- Scissors

- Felt-tip pens or crayons

Stick a quantity of blank people shapes on to the tree. Replenish later, as required.

Reflect: Consider those areas of your life, ministry, work or spiritual growth where you feel small, inadequate or not up to the job. Reflect on them honestly as you look at the tree and think about the story of Zacchaeus.

Pray: When you feel ready, respond by removing one of the people shapes from the tree, as a sign that you want God to help you to come down from your 'tree' and serve him, however small you feel.

Decorate the figure as yourself, praying as you do so. When your 'Zacchaeus' is finished, take it away with you as a reminder that God can and does do big things when we give our lives to him.

Place your Zacchaeus somewhere where you will see it regularly, to remind you to continue to ask God to help you as you seek to serve him.

Saul/Paul: trust in a transforming God

Prayer focus: To reflect on the story of Paul's conversion after encountering Jesus, and to bring our own prayers for restoration and renewal to a God who can transform lives.

 Bible reflection: *All those who heard him were astonished and asked, 'Isn't he the man who caused havoc in Jerusalem among those who call on this name? ... Yet Saul grew more and more powerful and baffled the Jews living in Damascus by proving that Jesus is the Messiah.* ACTS 9:21–22

What I need

- Blindfold or opaque scarf (sleeping masks are ideal)
- Desk lamp or candles
- Matches (if using candles)
- Small tealight candles, unlit

Reflect: Sit for a moment and reflect on areas of your life where you feel a particular need for God to shine the light of his love and grace afresh. Consider where you need God to bring transformation in your life or the lives of people known to you. This might include transformation in relationships, habits, personality traits or struggles with forgiveness.

Pray: Put on a blindfold and sit in darkness as you consider the things you would like God to illuminate or transform. Use these moments of 'blindness' to inspire your prayers.

When you are ready, commit your prayers to God, trusting his transforming power, and remove the blindfold. Appreciate the light and vision you now have and turn on the lamp or light a candle, as a sign that you are asking God to shine into the areas of life that you have considered.

Take a small tealight away with you, unlit, as a reminder of your prayer. You may wish to light it at home, as a reminder of God's light in dark times and his transforming grace.

Chapter 2

Women of faith

Hannah: patient faith

Prayer focus: To reflect on the story of Hannah and to pray for patience and an understanding of God's timing in your life. To help develop patient faith or give thanks for prayers answered after a time of waiting.

 Bible reflection: *So in the course of time Hannah became pregnant and gave birth to a son. She named him Samuel, saying, 'Because I asked the Lord for him.'*
1 SAMUEL 1:20

What I need

- Pencils or pens

- Cut-out clock faces with the words of 1 Samuel 1:20 printed on the reverse, plus space to write a prayer or word of hope or faith.

Lay out the clock faces on a table or board, with pens or pencils ready for use.

Reflect: Reflect on situations in your life that require patience, such as difficult circumstances, ongoing illness or a long-held prayer that has not yet been answered.

Pray: Use the verse printed on the clock face to inspire your prayers, thinking especially of those things that you need to trust in God to fulfil or deal with in due time. Pray for patience as you wait for an answer. Pray that God may bring clarity and peace as you continue to seek his assistance.

Take up a clock face as a reminder that God does things in due time—and trust the timing into his care.

Mary and Martha: rest and renewal

Prayer focus: To spend time resting at the feet of Jesus; being still in his presence and praying for openess to hear him speak; taking time to listen, as Mary did, and to be refreshed.

 Bible reflection: *Martha opened her home to him. She had a sister called Mary, who sat at the Lord's feet listening to what he said.*
LUKE 10:38–39

What I need

- Blanket, cushion or comfortable chair

- Tea and squash; cakes or biscuits

- Printed version of stories Jesus told, or Bibles open to the relevant passages

- Teabag to take home, with Bible verse attached

Reflect: Get settled on the chair, cushion or blanket after helping yourself to a drink and some cake or biscuits—and relax. While you relax, begin to reflect and draw near to God. Put aside the cares of the day—your work, your responsibilities—and take time for yourself. Try to switch from being a 'Martha' to resting in 'Mary' mode. Imagine yourself resting at the feet of your Lord.

Read a story or passage from the Bibles provided. You could reread a favourite or discover a new one.

Meditate on significant moments in your walk with God so far, for which you are thankful. Rest in God's presence and consider areas where you need to ask for God's strength and support.

Pray: Pray quietly, bringing to God your burdens, worries and joys, and any other issues that you feel led to mention.

Take time to listen to what God may have to say to you, giving some moments of quiet simply to waiting for him.

Only when you feel ready, stand, and leave with God any worries or burdens. Take away with you the sense of peace that you may have felt while you were relaxing as 'Mary'. Try to remember this feeling when you are in 'Martha' mode.

Also take away a teabag. When you stop for a cup of tea, another time, remember again to rest in God's presence and think of sitting at his feet.

Ruth: sacrificial living

Prayer focus: To reflect on the story of Ruth, who acted sacrificially towards Naomi; to pray about areas of our lives where we may need to put ourselves out for others.

 Bible reflection: *But Ruth replied, 'Don't urge me to leave you or to turn back from you. Where you go I will go, and where you stay I will stay'... The women said to Naomi, 'Praise be to the Lord, who this day has not left you without a guardian-redeemer.'*
RUTH 1:16; 4:14

What I need

- Pens

- Cardboard

- Bible open to the book of Ruth, or a printed version of the story

- Sandal shapes pre-cut from card, with the words of Ruth 4:14 printed on one side.

Reflect: Think about the things you may need to give up in order to live more fully a life of sacrificial love for others. Consider ways in which God has been your personal 'guardian-redeemer', as Boaz was to Ruth.

Ruth did not take the easy option, but trusted that she would find contentment in fulfilling her vow to forsake her own happiness in order to comfort Naomi. Think about areas of your life where God may be asking you to live more sacrificially. How could you invest more time in others? What might you need to entrust to God's redeeming power?

Pray: Bring all these thoughts to God in prayer. Know that God can help you live sacrificially as you entrust your life to him afresh.

As a sign that you are renewing your faith in your redeemer God, take up a sandal shape to represent your acceptance of his promise to protect and keep you.

In the same way that Boaz committed himself to caring for Ruth and being her protector, know that God promises to be your guardian-redeemer and will honour your sacrificial acts.

The widow's mite: giving our all

Prayer focus: To reflect on the story of the widow's mite and to pray for God's guidance to help us use our small resources to do big things in God's kingdom.

 Bible reflection: *He also saw a poor widow put in two very small copper coins. 'Truly I tell you,' he said, 'this poor widow has put in more than all the others. All these people gave their gifts out of their wealth; but she out of her poverty put in all she had to live on.'*
LUKE 21:2–4

What I need

- Foil-covered chocolate coins or shiny coins (for example, pennies)

- Yellow or white cardboard, cut into round coin shapes (palm sized)

- Small offering plate or tray

- Pens

- Luke 21:2–4 printed on paper

Reflect: Meditate on the story of the widow's mite. Consider the things you feel are worthless in your life and remind yourself that God can use them. They might include your time, kindness, words, gifts of hospitality or finances.

Pray: Take a cardboard coin shape and hold it in your hand as you pray. Pray about those gifts that you consider 'small' and ask God to use them to do significant things for his kingdom. Offer to God your time, prayers, talents and finances, including those areas of your life that feel insignificant.

Ask God to help you overcome feelings of unworthiness and show you ways in which you can serve him.

When you are ready, write a prayer on a cardboard coin, and add it to the offering plate. Leave it there as a response.

Take with you a chocolate coin or shiny coin, using it as a reminder of how God can use everything we give to him, however small we feel our offering might be.

Chapter 3

Miracles

Water into wine

Prayer focus: Using the story of Jesus' miracle at Cana, to give thanks and praise for the miracles we have seen in our own lives. We pray to a God who can do the impossible as we trust in the power of his Holy Spirit.

 Bible reflection: *What Jesus did here in Cana of Galilee was the first of the signs through which he revealed his glory; and his disciples believed in him.*
JOHN 2:11

What I need

- Non-clear plastic cups with a small amount of blackcurrant cordial in each

- Clear plastic water jug, filled with tap water

Reflect: Consider those issues, situations or people in your life that seem impossible, for which only a miracle from God could make a difference. Reflect on times in your past when God has done something that was beyond belief and truly made a difference.

Pray: When you are ready, pour some clear tap water into a plastic cup. Look into the cup to see that it is now filled with 'wine'.

Pray as you drink and enjoy, giving to God areas of your life where you feel a miracle is needed. These situations might include illness, relationships, past hurts or other circumstances personal to you or to someone you know.

Trust that God has heard your prayer and is already at work in the situation as you draw near to him in faith.

Miracle catch

Prayer focus: Using the story of the miraculous catch of fish, pray for obedience as we trust God to help us 'cast our nets' and guide our thinking.

 Bible reflection: *When [Jesus] had finished speaking, he said to Simon, 'Put out into deep water, and let down the nets for a catch.' Simon answered, 'Master, we've worked hard all night and haven't caught anything. But because you say so, I will let down the nets.' When they had done so, they caught such a large number of fish that their nets began to break.*

LUKE 5:4–6

What I need

- A large piece of netting (such as a fishing net or similar) or a net drawn on a large piece of paper or card

- Silver foil or metallic cardboard cut into fish shapes

- Address labels

- Pens

- Pegs or sticky tape

Reflect: Consider the story of the miraculous catch achieved when the disciples trusted Jesus and cast their nets on the other side of the boat. How could you obediently trust God in your life and potentially reap a 'catch' far larger than you can imagine ?

Pray: Write a prayer on a fish shape—perhaps a prayer of obedience about placing your life and future path into God's care.

Give thanks for those times when God has already done more than you thought possible and helped you gain a miracle 'catch' in your life, work or ministry.

When you are ready, stick or peg your prayer fish on to the net, as a sign that you trust God to guide you in your 'fishing' and provide all that you need.

At the end of the event, see how participants have created their very own 'miracle catch' together—a net full of prayer fish.

Raising of Lazarus: 'bandage' prayer

Prayer focus: Using the story of Lazurus, to remember that God can bring life to circumstances that seem dead or hopeless, joy even in times of struggle, and hope in even our darkest days.

 Bible reflection: *When he had said this, Jesus called in a loud voice, 'Lazarus, come out!' The dead man came out, his hands and feet wrapped with strips of linen, and a cloth round his face. Jesus said to them, 'Take off the grave clothes and let him go.'*
JOHN 11:43–44

What I need

- Strips of fabric or actual fabric bandages, unrolled

- Small individual fabric plasters

- Pens (for example, markers) suitable for writing on the bandage

Reflect: Consider the story of Jesus raising Lazarus from the dead. Reflect on those circumstances in your life that seem 'dead', without hope of restoration. Know that God has the power to restore, renew and encourage you and wants you to feel his power to perform miracles or bring hope.

Pray: Pray about whatever has come to mind for you, where you or someone you know needs God's miracle-working power and strength.

When you feel ready, write a prayer on the bandage. It could be a full prayer or simply a name, a word or a small drawing.

While you write your prayer, give to God those areas of life that feel damaged or beyond repair, and think of the bandage as symbolising your faith in God's healing strength and perfect peace.

Take a small plaster and stick it on your clothes or a place where you will see it regularly, as a reminder of your prayer and your trust in God's power to heal and restore.

Stepping out of the boat

Prayer focus: We often feel afraid, just as Peter did, and need God's help to step out in faith in many areas of our lives. This prayer provides an opportunity to give our fears to God, to 'step out of the boat' with him and to give thanks for times when he has helped us to move out of our comfort zone.

 Bible reflection: *Then Peter got down out of the boat, walked on the water and came towards Jesus. But when he saw the wind, he was afraid and, beginning to sink, cried out, 'Lord, save me!' Immediately Jesus reached out his hand and caught him.*
MATTHEW 14:29–31

What I need

- Large blue blanket, sheet or piece of cloth to spread on the floor
- A selection of scatter cushions or beanbags

Place the cushions or beanbags on the sheet or blanket, to represent boats on the sea.

Reflect: Is there an area of your life where you need God's help to step out in faith? Consider the circumstances in which you need God's strength and the courage that only he can provide.

Find a comfortable 'boat' to sit on and spend some time reflecting on the ways in which you need God's help to 'step out'.

Pray: Pray about any issues you find frightening or that seem beyond your ability or outside your comfort zone.

When you feel ready, commit these issues to God and stand up, stepping out of your 'boat' into the surrounding 'sea' as a sign that you are trusting God to help you step out in faith.

You may also wish to pray a prayer of thanksgiving for those times in your life when God has already helped you to do something you thought was impossible and enabled you to step out of the boat.

Chapter 4

Bible promises

Prayer for hope

Prayer focus: Using Jeremiah 29:11, to reflect on and pray about God's promise to sustain us and give us hope, reminding ourselves to trust in his plans for our lives.

 Bible reflection: *'For I know the plans I have for you,' declares the Lord, 'plans to prosper you and not to harm you, plans to give you hope and a future.'*
JEREMIAH 29:11

What I need

- Bibles open at Jeremiah 29:11 (you may want to use a few different translations)

- A selection of objects including the words of Jeremiah 29:11—for example, fridge magnets, postcards or bookmarks (available from Christian bookshops)

- Small decorative copies of the verse printed on cardboard, in a size that fits into a purse or wallet

Reflect: Reflect on those areas of your life that are currently a struggle, and offer them in prayer to the God who promises to give you hope and a future. Think about the times when, with hindsight, you can see that God was at work, and give thanks.

Pray: Read Jeremiah 29:11 again in the different versions provided. Pray the words through as you read them, slowly. They may be very familiar, so take time to concentrate on them and on what they mean to you personally.

When you are ready, use the verse to guide your prayers of request and thanksgiving for current needs and for times in the past when God has revealed his plans for your life.

Give thanks to God for the hope found in trusting him and ask him to give a sense of this hope to others known to you who may be feeling uncertainty or despair.

Ask God to make Jeremiah 29:11 real in your everyday life or current struggles. Take a small printed card away with you, using it as a reminder of your time of prayer and an encouragement to continue to trust in God. You could think about giving it to someone who particularly needs its encouragement at the moment.

Prayer for strength

Prayer focus: To find renewal and fresh strength by resting in God's presence; to take time to reflect on his promise of rest for the weary soul.

 Bible reflection: *'Come to me, all you who are weary and burdened, and I will give you rest. Take my yoke upon you and learn from me, for I am gentle and humble in heart, and you will find rest for your souls.'*
MATTHEW 11:28–29

What I need

• Assorted comfy chairs, beanbags, cushions or blankets

• Bibles or printed copies of Matthew 11:28–29

• Small cards printed with the words of the verses

Reflect: God promises to provide rest for the weary and to comfort those who place their burdens in his care. Consider the 'burdens' you may be struggling to carry alone and admit that you need to relinquish them to God.

Pray: Find a comfortable place to sit, choosing a chair, beanbag, cushion or space to suit you.

Spend some time silently resting in God's presence. Let your daily concerns go, or name them in prayer and give them over to God. Take some time to stop, be still, rest and prayerfully commit your burdens into his hands.

Try to still your mind, letting go of any concerns and your awareness of time passing. Focus purely on God and use the Bible verse provided to aid your prayer and reflection, if desired.

When you feel ready, stand up, leaving your burdens with God and trusting him for the strength you need.

Take a small printed card as a reminder of your prayers and to aid your quiet reflection at other times.

Prayer for peace

Prayer focus: To ask God for a renewed sense of peace, regardless of our circumstances. To know God's comfort, even in the midst of our fears and in times of trouble.

 Bible reflection: *'I am leaving you with a gift—peace of mind and heart. And the peace I give is a gift the world cannot give. So don't be troubled or afraid.'*
JOHN 14:27 (NLT)

What I need

- Bibles or printed copies of John 14:27

- Either pebbles or cardboard cut into heart shapes

- Pens that will write on the materials used

- Giftwrap (optional)

Write the word 'peace' on each cardboard heart or pebble. You might like to wrap each one in giftwrap as a gift of peace.

Reflect: Meditate on God's peace, thinking about ways in which you need a renewed sense of calm and rest. Read John 14:27 and consider the gift of peace that God gives, that the world cannot provide.

Pray: When you have read the verse and reflected, begin to pray about those areas of your life where you need to feel God's peace, which surpasses human understanding and transcends our circumstances.

Pick up a 'gift' of peace and hold it as you pray. Look at it in your hand and give thanks to God for the gift of his peace.

Prayerfully commit yourself to trying to remember this gift and to living in the knowledge of God's peace, whatever your circumstances.

Give thanks to God for the peace of mind, heart and spirit that he has given you already, and ask for a renewal of this peace now, for yourself and others known to you who are in need.

Take your gift of peace away with you and use it to remind you of God's promise. Place it somewhere where you will see it regularly or give it as a gift to someone who you know needs God's peace.

Prayer for joy

Prayer focus: To pray for strength and joy and to give all our griefs and worries over to God. To use scripture and lyrics based on scripture to inspire and comfort us in times of difficulty.

 Bible reflection: *'Do not grieve, for the joy of the Lord is your strength.'*
NEHEMIAH 8:10

What I need

- Bibles or printed copies of Nehemiah 8:10

- Copies of the lyrics of relevant worship songs or CD/MP3 versions of the songs—for example, 'Holy is the Lord' by Chris Tomlin (optional)

- Headphones and audio equipment (optional)

Reflect: In tough times, it is hard to feel joy and to have strength. Often we fear that we cannot regain the happiness we have experienced in good times, perhaps when we first encountered God. Think about tough times you have known, either current or past, and also about God's joy, which is beyond our understanding. Reflect on Nehemiah 8:10, which promises God's help to keep us strong. Bring to mind others who may particularly need to know the joy and strength that God provides.

Pray: Look again at this familiar Bible verse, or reflect on the lyrics that use this scripture.

Pray for a renewal of your strength, commiting your life, your worries and grief into God's hands. Ask him to fill you with the strength to persevere and a sense of joy, whatever your circumstances.

Bring to God in prayer others known to you who may be in need of his promise and a fresh sense of joy or strength.

However weak you feel, trust as you pray that God's joy can be your sustaining strength.

Section 2

Walking in our world

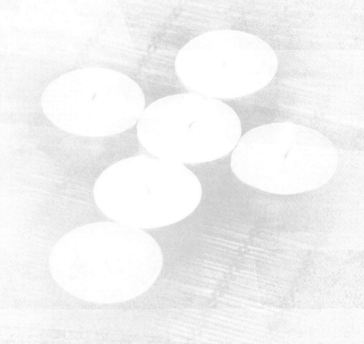

Chapter 5

Praying with water

Water of life

Prayer focus: Using bottled water, to reflect on the 'living water' that Jesus gives freely to all who draw near to God; to pray for refreshment and quenching of our spiritual thirst.

 Bible reflection: *Jesus answered, 'Everyone who drinks this water will be thirsty again, but whoever drinks the water I give them will never thirst. Indeed, the water I give them will become in them a spring of water welling up to eternal life.'*
JOHN 4:13–14

What I need

- Bibles or printed copies of John 4:13–14

- Individual small bottles of still mineral water

- Large white address labels

- Marker pens

- Handwriting pens

- Water droplet shapes cut out of cardboard (pale blue or white)

Write 'living water' on to an address label with a marker pen and stick it over the brand label of each bottle.

Reflect: Read the verses from John 4 and reflect on areas of your life and faith where you feel you need refreshing and rejuvenating with the living water of Jesus to sustain you.

Pray: Take a bottle of 'living water'. As you drink the clear, pure water, pray about the restorative, cleansing 'living water' that Jesus promises.

Give thanks for the times when you have known this refreshment in the past and ask God to give you a sense of renewal and a quenching of your spiritual thirst as you drink.

Bring to God, with honesty, anything in your spiritual life or ministry that feels 'dry' and in need of his cleansing power.

Write a prayer on a water droplet shape, as a sign that you accept the living water he offers.

When you are ready and feel refreshed, move on. Take your water bottle and droplet as reminders of God's promise and your prayers.

Parting of the Red Sea

Prayer focus: To pray for God's help in overcoming seemingly impossible obstacles and giving to God anything that feels overwhelming.

 Bible reflection: *Jesus looked at them and said, 'With human beings this is impossible, but with God all things are possible.'*
MATTHEW 19:26 (TNIV)

What I need

- Tap water

- Tray or bowl

- Drinking straws (for single use)

- Plastic tablecloth

Cover your table with a waterproof tablecloth and pour a small amount of water into the tray so that it just covers the bottom. Test the station beforehand to ensure that the water 'parts' when blown on with a straw but doesn't spill excessively.

Reflect: Think about a circumstance that feels insurmountable, like the crossing of the Red Sea. Look at the water in front of you and consciously place your trust in the God who can even part the seas.

Pray: Take up a fresh straw and begin to bring to God any issues that feel impossible in your life, faith or ministry. At the same time, blow gently with the straw on the surface of the water.

Commit your worries to God as you watch the water part, trusting God to help you overcome the challenges you face.

Give thanks to God for the times in your Christian walk when he made a way for you where no progress seemed humanly possible.

Take your straw with you as a reminder of God's miracle-working strength.

Jesus calms the storm

Prayer focus: Using a practical demonstration of waves, to respond in prayer to God who can calm the storms in our lives.

 Bible reflection: *The disciples went and woke him, saying, 'Master, Master, we're going to drown!' He got up and rebuked the wind and the raging waters; the storm subsided, and all was calm.*

LUKE 8:24

What I need

- Large blue cloth (organza or similar light cloth, or a thin sheet, is ideal)

- Blue fabric cut up into small squares

Lay the cloth out flat on the floor, allowing plenty of space around the edge for a person or many people to sit or stand.

This prayer can be done silently or aloud, individually or as part of a whole group.

Reflect: Consider those areas of life that are currently 'stormy', difficult or frightening, whether for yourself or others. Think of circumstances that you yourself or others known to you are experiencing, in which God's hope and grace are needed to calm the storm.

Pray: Individually or as a group, sit or stand at the edge of the cloth 'sea'.

Begin to shake the cloth silently, to create waves. As you do so, pray about those areas of life that feel stormy and out of control. Continue to pray, giving your fears over to God by imagining that you are casting them into the waves.

Next, hold the cloth absolutely still, watching as the waves you created start to settle. Use this image of calm to inspire prayers of thanksgiving for the way God has calmed other storms in your life, or to confirm your trust in a God who has the power to bring calm in your current storms.

When you are ready, replace the 'sea' flat on the floor, leaving your concerns in God's hands and taking with you a small piece of blue fabric. Put this somewhere where it will continue to remind you of God's strength in times of trouble.

Jesus washes the disciples' feet

Prayer focus: Using the story of Jesus washing the disciples' feet, to pray about how we can consider others' needs and take action humbly to put others before ourselves.

 Bible reflection: *After that, he poured water into a basin and began to wash his disciples' feet, drying them with the towel that was wrapped around him. He came to Simon Peter, who said to him, 'Lord, are you going to wash my feet?' Jesus replied, 'You do not realise now what I am doing, but later you will understand.'*
JOHN 13:5–7

What I need

- Bible or printed copy of John 13:5–7
- Large plastic bowl, such as a washing-up bowl or larger, half full of tap water
- Tiny foot shapes cut from coloured craft foam (in skin tones)
- Scissors
- Waterproof sheet or tablecloth
- Paper towels

Set up the station with a waterproof sheet under the bowl, and paper towels ready, and place a quantity of foot shapes near the bowl.

Reflect: Jesus teaches us, by his actions, to consider others. Reflect on ways you can humbly support others, or times when you may have neglected to do so.

Pray: Pray about ways in which you can put others first, or ask for forgiveness for the times when you have failed to think of others. As a commitment to trying to follow Jesus' example in your own life, respond by placing a foam foot shape in the water.

Leave the foot floating in the water for a moment as you reflect and pray. When you are ready, take the foot that you have 'washed' out of the bowl. Use this action as a sign that you are determined to take care to consider others and pray regularly for God's direction in the best ways to act for others.

Dry the foam foot on a paper towel and take it away with you as a reminder to act humbly to help others, as Jesus did.

Chapter 6

Wind prayers

Fan ribbons

Prayer focus: Using colourful ribbons and a fan, to pray for a renewal of strength and a fresh infilling of energy from God's Holy Spirit.

 Bible reflection: *Restore to me the joy of your salvation and grant me a willing spirit, to sustain me.*
PSALM 51:12

What I need

- Lengths of coloured ribbon

- A large electric fan (with grill casing)

Plug the fan in, switched to 'off'. Place a selection of ribbons next to the fan.

Reflect: Consider how God enables us to continue our walk with him, even when we tire. Think about areas of your life, work, health or ministry where you feel physically, emotionally or spiritually weary.

Pray: Begin to bring your concerns to God in prayer. Choose a ribbon and tie it on to the grill casing of the fan (still switched off).

Look at the ribbon, securely fixed but weak and limp, and pray for areas of your life that need a fresh infilling of God's Spirit to energise you, to help you feel connected to him again.

When you are ready, respond by switching on the fan. Pray as you watch your ribbon flutter energetically in the wind produced by the fan, giving thanks to God for his power and strength.

Sit for a moment and feel the air blowing on to your face. Use this sensation to remind you of God's Spirit refreshing you spiritually.

When you are ready, turn the fan off and leave your ribbon tied on the casing as a sign that you are leaving your weariness with God. When you walk away, recall the sensation of the breeze on your face, remembering that God sends his Spirit to renew our strength.

Bubbles

Prayer focus: To reflect on the unique beauty of bubbles and to use this image to inspire prayers of thanksgiving for God's created world, our unique gifts and the chance to spread God's love.

 Bible reflection: *I praise you because I am fearfully and wonderfully made; your works are wonderful, I know that full well.*
PSALM 139:14

What I need

- Tubs of bubble mixture or toy bubble machine

- Wipes or cloths to clean the floor if it becomes slippery

Check in advance that your venue allows bubbles to be used, or set up the station out of doors if possible.
    Ensure that the station is monitored and any spills cleaned up.

Reflect: Bubbles are amazing and unique, just like each of us. When they are caught by the wind, they are not only a beautiful sight to behold, but can really travel far. Blow some bubbles and watch them as they float, powered by your breath, each one different from the others.

Pray: Watch the bubbles and begin to pray. Reflect on each bubble's unique size and path as it floats. Bring before God your unique gifts and give thanks for them and for the purposes God has set for you.

Pray for inspiration to know how you can be used by God to spread his love in the world. Watch the bubbles float away and burst, then commit your prayers to God, asking for a fresh infilling of his 'breath' to help you do all he has called you to do as you go out into the world.

Prayer spinner

Prayer focus: Using a paper prayer spinner, to offer prayers to God as it flutters to the ground, buoyed up by the air around it.

 Bible reflection: *So I turned to the Lord God and pleaded with him in prayer and petition… I prayed to the Lord my God.*
DANIEL 9:3–4

What I need

- Paper prayer spinners, either pre-cut or as printed templates with instructions (see page 188)

- Scissors (if you are cutting out the spinners as part of the activity)

- Paperclips

- Pens

Make sure there is plenty of space at the station to stand and drop the prayer spinners in response.

Reflect: Letting go of problems or releasing our requests to God can be difficult at times, whatever the stage of our faith journey. Consider what you need to give to God in prayer, perhaps in an act of confession or letting God take control.

Pray: Take a paper prayer spinner and write a prayer on the blades. Decorate it if you wish and spend time asking God to help you let go and allow him to work in your life.

When you are ready, fold the blades in opposite directions from each other and attach a paperclip to the tip as a weight. Fold your prayer spinner blades flat, like a helicopter, and hold it firmly by the long middle section, at arm's length.

When you are ready, commit your prayers to God and, as an act of letting go, release your prayer spinner and watch it rotate towards the ground, carrying your prayers with it.

Pinwheels

Prayer focus: To reflect on God's power to bring about change through his transforming Holy Spirit, which can move us into action for him.

 Bible reflection: *And with that he breathed on them and said, 'Receive the Holy Spirit. If you forgive anyone's sins, their sins are forgiven; if you do not forgive them, they are not forgiven.'*
JOHN 20:22–23

What I need

- Pre-cut paper pinwheels with small holes punched in the corners and a small hole cut in the middle (see template and instructions on page 189)
- Pens and felt-tip pens
- Scissors
- Sticky tack
- Bendy plastic drinking straws

Reflect: God's awesome power, through the gift of his Holy Spirit, can bring change, just as a person's breath can move a pinwheel. Consider changes that God has helped you make in your life already or changes that you need his help to make in your personal, work or faith life.

Pray: On the points of the pinwheel, write a prayer of thanks or action, or names of people who need a special infilling of God's Spirit. You may also wish to decorate it, using the pens provided. Use this creative time to pray through the things you have reflected on, bringing them to God.

When your pinwheel is finished, push the short, bendy section of a straw through the hole in the middle. One by one, bring the holed corners of the pinwheel into the middle, sliding them on to the straw, so the holes are on top of each other. Lastly, fix a blob of sticky tack to the end of the straw, securing the pinwheel but leaving the blades loose enough to allow it to spin around.

As you blow the pinwheel round, watch the words and design blur before your eyes, powered by your breath. Watch it twirl and commit your prayers to God.

Keep your pinwheel as a reminder to keep on asking God for his Holy Spirit and power to make positive changes in your life and the lives of others.

Chapter 7

Praying with the seasons

Autumn leaves

Prayer focus: Using actual fallen leaves or cardboard leaves, to pray for God's help to shed whatever hinders us from reaching our God-given potential, as a tree sheds its leaves.

 Bible reflection: *Therefore, since we are surrounded by such a great cloud of witnesses, let us throw off everything that hinders and the sin that so easily entangles. And let us run with perseverance the race marked out for us.*
HEBREWS 12:1

What I need

- Fallen autumn leaves or orange and brown cardboard leaves

- Extra, smaller cardboard leaves

- Real branches or twigs, or brown cardboard cut into twig/branch shapes

- Vase or other container

Place the branches or twigs in their vase on your station, with leaves (real or cardboard) scattered around the base, plus an additional pile of smaller card leaf shapes.

Reflect: Autumn can be a sad time, with trees losing leaves and cold weather coming. However, fallen leaves can also be used to represent hope and new beginnings, a sign of having cast off the old ways and looking forward to the promise of new growth and life.

Pray: Spend some time looking at the autumn leaves at the base of the 'tree'. Use them to inspire you in prayers of thankfulness to God for those things he has helped you shed from your life, which hindered you in your walk with him.

Pray also for those things that you would still like to shed. You may pick up a fallen leaf and hold it as you pray. Give to God whatever you feel is holding you back—your fears, regrets, guilt, hurts or habits, and ask that he will help you have the strength to shed them.

When you are ready, commit these prayers to God and lay the leaf down by the tree as a sign of letting go. Pick up a small cardboard leaf to keep as a reminder of your prayers.

Winter ice

Prayer focus: To pray for strength and perseverance to endure times of 'winter' in our life; to seek God in the seasons of our faith when life is a struggle and 'spring' seems far away.

 Bible reflection: *The Lord is good to those whose hope is in him, to the one who seeks him; it is good to wait quietly for the salvation of the Lord.*
LAMENTATIONS 3:25–26

What I need

- Warm tap water (not boiling) in a plastic bowl
- Ice cubes in another plastic bowl
- Plastic tablecloth

Place both bowls on your station, with a plastic tablecloth underneath them. You will need both to change the warm water as it cools and to add fresh ice cubes, particularly for a longer prayer event.

Reflect: Winter can seem endless, but it can be a lesson in patience as we await the coming of spring. It is also the season when we celebrate Jesus' birth—the fulfilment of a long-awaited prophecy. Consider any issues in your life that seem to go unresolved or in which change seems impossible. Even when we feel as if we are enduring a winter season in our faith, God is still at work and can help us to be patient as we wait for spring.

Pray: Pray about those issues that seem frozen and hard to change in your life. Pick up an ice cube and pray about 'icy' or difficult circumstances or relationships as you briefly feel the cold cube in your hand.

After a moment, place the ice cube into the bowl of warm water and watch as it slowly melts.

Take some time to consider the things for which you are waiting, and ask God for the patience you need. Trust that God will hold you through the winter seasons of your life and that there is always the promise of spring and new beginnings with God. Sometimes this is a slow process, just like the melting of ice, and you may have to remind yourself, as you wait for winter to end, that the season will surely change one day.

Spring flowers

Prayer focus: Spring is a time to celebrate new life, fresh starts and hope. This is a prayer of thanksgiving for new beginnings with God. It can also be a chance to pray for God's guidance if you are seeking some kind of fresh start.

 Bible reflection: *Therefore, if anyone is in Christ, the new creation has come: the old has gone, the new is here!*
2 CORINTHIANS 5:17

What I need

- Tissue paper in various bright colours, pre-cut into circles or petal shapes

- Split-pin fasteners

- A large green sheet or rug, or even a piece of real turf, if available

Reflect: Consider the vibrant colours of the tissue paper and choose some petal shapes to make a flower. As you do this, reflect on the new life all around us during spring, the promise of change and hope reflected in nature.

Pray: Take your petal shapes and layer them, then fix them together with a split-pin fastener. Pray a prayer of thanksgiving for something new that God has begun to grow in your life, or pray about a circumstance in which you feel there is a need for a fresh start with God or a renewed vibrancy in your walk with him.

Make the securing of the petals a confirmation that you are giving these things over to God in prayer, and place the tissue paper flower on the rug or sheet as a symbol of this commitment.

Summer sand

Prayer focus: To use sand as a link to the theme of summer as a time for rest and refreshment; to pray for renewal and forgiveness for anything holding you back in your walk with God.

 Bible reflection: *'Therefore, I tell you, her many sins have been forgiven—as her great love has shown. But whoever has been forgiven little loves little.' Then Jesus said to her, 'Your sins are forgiven.'*
LUKE 7:47–48

What I need

- A shallow tray, filled with soft sand (not builder's sand), deep enough to draw in

- Plastic sheet or tablecloth

Place the plastic sheet or tablecloth under the sand tray.

Reflect: Summer is usually a time for holidays and fun but also offers a chance to reflect on anything for which you may need to seek forgiveness. Consider what you wish to bring before God— things you know are wrong or unhelpful and prevent you living to the full the life that God has for you.

Pray: Pray through these issues and, as you do so, write a word or draw something in the tray of sand. Use this as a prayer of confession between you and God, made visible in the sand. When you are ready, ask God for forgiveness and shake the tray so that your word or drawing disappears.

God promises that when we repent, our sins are obliterated in the same way. Know that you can start afresh with God and he will not remember those sins. Just as there is now no trace left of what you wrote in the sand, so God promises that there will be no trace of our confessed sins when we truly repent. Leave the tray as you found it and remember that you are free to live in forgiveness through God's grace.

Chapter 8

Fruit of the Spirit

Fruit tree

Prayer focus: To pray creatively for an increase in your life of the fruit of the Holy Spirit; to ask for God's help to develop this fruit in your life.

 Bible reflection: *But the fruit of the Spirit is love, joy, peace, patience, kindness, goodness, faithfulness, gentleness and self-control. Against such things there is no law.*
GALATIANS 5:22–23 (TNIV)

What I need

- Tree twigs or a whole small branch or a cardboard tree outline

- Vase or similar container

- Fruit shapes (apple, pear, banana, orange) cut from green, yellow, red and orange paper, with a hole punched in each one

- Pens

- Ribbons or string

Set up a 'tree' of twigs in a vase with fruit shapes nearby, plus ribbons or string, and pens.

Reflect: Consider what aspects of the fruit of the Spirit you would like more of in your life. Do you need more patience or self-control or to show kindness more readily to others? Think also of the fruit that God has given you already to help you do his will in the world, for which you can be thankful.

Pray: When you are ready, choose a fruit from the selection of paper outlines. Take some time to pray about whatever aspect of the fruit of the Holy Spirit you need, and write a prayer on the paper fruit. You may want to write a single word, such as 'patience' or 'peace', or a full prayer.

Spend a few moments asking God for more of the fruit of the Spirit in your life. Then add your fruit prayer on to a branch of the tree, creating a tree filled with the fruit of the Spirit.

Leave your fruit with all the others and know that God truly can fill you with the fruit of the Holy Spirit to help you in your faith and actions day by day.

Fruit juice

Prayer focus: To reflect on the refreshment that we can receive when we are filled afresh, or the first time, with the fruit of God's Holy Spirit; to pray for the qualities mentioned in Galatians 5:22–23: love, joy, peace, patience, kindness, goodness, faithfulness, gentleness and self-control.

 Bible reflection: *Since we live by the Spirit, let us keep in step with the Spirit.*
GALATIANS 5:25

What I need

- Fruit juice (for example, apple, orange, tropical juices)
- Disposable plastic or paper cups
- Sticky address labels
- Marker pen
- Small cards
- Plastic tablecloth

Use the marker pen to write a single fruit of the Spirit on each label (for example, 'love', 'patience', 'peace', 'joy') and fix the labels to the plastic or paper cups in advance.

Provide several cups for each 'fruit' type.

On the small cards, write or print either single fruits of the Spirit or Galatians 5:22–23 in full for people to take away.

Reflect: Consider the fruit of the Holy Spirit mentioned in Galatians 5:22–23, and think about which of them you most need in your life. You may want to ask God for a fresh experience of peace or patience, or for a refilling of one of the qualities that you know you struggle to live out, like self-control or gentleness.

Pray: As you begin to pray, take a cup labelled with the fruit of the Spirit that you feel you want more of in your life. Pour some fruit juice into your cup. Drink the refreshing juice and pray about your desire to grow or cultivate this fruit in your life.

Relax and allow God's Spirit to fill you afresh as you enjoy the fruit juice. When you have finished, take your cup with you along with a small Galatians 5 card, to prompt you to keep on asking God to help you develop the fruit of the Spirit.

Fruit bowl

Prayer focus: To ask God for more of the fruit of the Holy Spirit to enable you in your walk with him; to give thanks for all that he has already freely given you.

 Bible reflection: *'God, who knows the heart, showed that he accepted them by giving the Holy Spirit to them, just as he did to us.'*
ACTS 15:8

What I need

- Selection of real or wax fruit, such as apples, bananas, oranges and pears

- Large fruit bowl or basket

- Marker pen

Prepare the fruits by writing a different fruit of the Spirit (as listed in Galatians 5:22–23) on the skin of each piece, written clearly in bold letters with the marker pen. Set up the fruit in the bowl or basket.

Reflect: God promises to give us freely the fruit of the Holy Spirit, by his grace and mercy. Sometimes we need to take hold of this fruit again in our lives and pray for a deeper consciousness of it at work or at home, especially those aspects of the fruit that we find harder to live out.

Pray: Sit comfortably and choose a piece of fruit from the bowl. Hold it and, as you read the word written on it, pray about this fruit of the Spirit in your life.

Give thanks to God that he gives us the fruit of the Holy Spirit freely. Ask him to help you with those aspects of the fruit that you struggle to sense as present in your daily life.

Feel free to take as many individual fruits as you want, to hold as you pray and reflect on the working of God's Spirit. As you replace each one in the bowl, pray that this action will help you to remember to keep on asking God to bless you with more of his Holy Spirit in order to grow that fruit in your life.

Fruit sweets

Prayer focus: To reflect and give thanks for the fruit of the Spirit demonstrated to us through the words and actions of others.

 Bible reflection: *There are different kinds of gifts, but the same Spirit distributes them. There are different kinds of service, but the same Lord. There are different kinds of working, but in all of them and in everyone it is the same God at work. Now to each one the manifestation of the Spirit is given for the common good.*
1 CORINTHIANS 12:4–7

What I need

- Large piece of cardboard with a tree outline drawn or printed on to it

- Selection of individually wrapped fruit-flavoured sweets in a small bowl

- Glue sticks

Reflect: Reflect on how the fruit of the Spirit can be seen in the words or actions of others around us. Consider individuals or organisations who demonstrate love, kindness, patience, joy, gentleness or other qualities, showing the fruit of the Spirit in their lives and making a difference for others.

Pray: Choose a sweet, unwrap it and eat it. As you enjoy the taste, scrunch the wrapper into a little ball as you give thanks to God for the fruit of his Spirit that others demonstrate, which makes a difference in your life or the lives of others in your community or the wider world.

When you are ready, glue the scrunched-up wrapper on to the tree outline to represent a fruit growing on one of the branches, as you pray for those who embody the fruit of God's Spirit.

You may like to take another sweet to give to the person you have been praying for, if they are known to you personally, as a gesture of thanks and to let them know that they are an example to you.

Section 3

Walking as a church

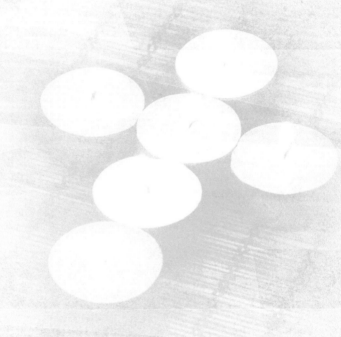

Chapter 9

Lent and Easter

Turning over a new leaf

Prayer focus: Lent and Easter are times of new life and fresh starts: flowers begin to grow and new life is evident all around us. As we prepare to celebrate Easter, we can also make a choice to make a fresh start or to turn over a new leaf in our lives, with God's help.

 Bible reflection: *Therefore, if anyone is in Christ, the new creation has come: the old has gone, the new is here!*
2 CORINTHIANS 5:17

What I need

- Leaf shapes cut out of green paper or thin card (use white paper if green is unavailable)

- Tray (optional)

- Pens

In bold print on the reverse of the leaf shapes, write some behaviours or areas of life that people may want to change (perhaps in their friendships, work or prayer life). Provide some blank leaves, to be written on as people feel led.

Place all the leaves on a table or tray, with the words facing down.

Reflect: Reflect on whether there is anything you would like to do differently in life—for example, a habit you would like to change.

Pray: Turn over the leaves one by one, and, if you find an area of your life in which you feel you need to 'turn over a new leaf', pray about that.

If you want to pray for something different, that isn't already printed on a leaf shape, write your own word or phrase on a blank leaf. You can then pray for a fresh start and turn over that new leaf instead.

Take your new leaf (or leaves) away with you as a reminder of your prayer.

As time goes on, you may need to return to this exercise, turning over a new leaf as often as you need.

Rolling back the stone

Prayer focus: Thinking of the stone rolled away from the tomb, to consider those things that may be blocking you from walking in freedom and living the new life that God has for you.

 Bible reflection: *We were therefore buried with him through baptism into death in order that, just as Christ was raised from the dead through the glory of the Father, we too may live a new life.*
ROMANS 6:4

What I need

- A selection of small stones (either pebbles you have collected or decorative pebbles available from homeware shops)
- A large bowl of water (not too deep)
- Waterproof sheet or tablecloth

Place the bowl of water and a selection of stones on the waterproof sheet or cloth.

Reflect: Is there something that prevents you from stepping out and living to the full the new life that God offers you? Are you held back by lies, hurt, anger, bitterness, unforgiveness or the memory of past events ?

Pray: Pray about the things that may be blocking you from embracing new life with God to the full. As you reflect on them in prayer, take up a stone and hold it in your hand. Release them to God and ask him to roll away the 'stone' in your life.

When you are ready, respond by placing your stone in the bowl of water. This is a symbol of committing your request to God and handing over to him whatever is troubling you.

'It's not like it used to be'

Prayer focus: To reflect on areas of faith that feel 'not like they used to be'; to ask God to help you regain, or discover for the first time, the joy of walking with him.

 Bible reflection: *Restore to me the joy of your salvation and grant me a willing spirit, to sustain me.*
PSALM 51:12

What I need

- Sweet and savoury snacks, such as crisps, mini chocolate bars and sweets, in small bowls

Reflect: People often comment, especially as they get older, how things in life are 'not like they used to be'. Favourite chocolate bars have become smaller or don't taste as good, and crisp packets seem half empty. Does your faith feel a bit like this sometimes? Is it not as 'big' as it used to be? Does it seem 'half full' or not as 'sweet' as you remember it once was?

Consider ways in which your relationship with God may have lost some of its sweetness over time.

Pray: As you eat some snacks, ask God to renew in you (or fill you for the first time) with the joy and 'sweetness' that so many people feel when they begin their journey of faith. Take time to think of ways to rediscover this joy.

If your faith feels half full or not as big as it used to, ask God to renew or refill you with his Holy Spirit over this Lent and Easter time as you take time to pray and reflect on your journey with him.

Faces of Jesus

Prayer focus: Using a variety of images of Jesus, to meditate on who Jesus is and to give thanks for all he has done in your life.

 Bible reflection: *Christ Jesus: who, being in very nature God, did not consider equality with God something to be used to his own advantage; rather, he made himself nothing by taking the very nature of a servant, being made in human likeness. And being found in appearance as a man, he humbled himself by becoming obedient to death— even death on a cross!'*

PHILIPPIANS 2:5–8

What I need

- Printed pictures or a continuous slideshow of images of Jesus, from film and art, on a laptop

- Table with a comfortable chair or chairs nearby

You can find plenty of varied depictions of Christ online or in books and other printed material. Include images from different times in Jesus' earthly life, including his death on the cross.

Reflect: Consider your own personal image of Jesus. When you read scripture, how do you imagine him looking? Was he blond or dark-haired? What colour do you imagine his eyes may have been? This image may be based on films, stained-glass windows or art images you have seen, or perhaps on long-held personal ideas of how Jesus may have looked.

Pray: Using your own ideas of the image of Christ and those provided, begin to pray to him as your Lord and Saviour, giving thanks for the things he has taught you as well as the stories he told and the man he was, as recorded in scripture.

As you look at the visual depictions that have been imagined by others, consider some ways in which you would like to deepen or renew your relationship with Jesus. Pray these through and ask him to guide you.

Meditate on the images of Jesus upon the cross—the painful, horrendous reality of his death—but also remember his rising in glory. Pray for a renewed sense of Jesus' resurrection power for you personally, and an understanding of how it can inform your onward journey with God. How might it affect the part you play in the body of Christ, your church, and your local community as you serve God where you are?

Chapter 10

Pentecost

Fire

Prayer focus: Using candles, to meditate upon God's light in our lives.; to pray for a re-igniting of faith and inspiration for ways to 'shine' God's love to the world.

 Bible reflection: *You, Lord, are my lamp; the Lord turns my darkness into light.*
2 SAMUEL 22:29

What I need

- Candles

- Matches

- Small tealight candles

Reflect: Consider how your faith is like a flame. Does it still burn as brightly as it used to? Does it need fanning into a stronger fire or does the flame need re-igniting because it has been all but extinguished ?

Pray: Take a candle and, as you look at the unlit wick, pray about your own flame of faith. Be honest with God about how brightly or dimly you feel your faith is burning currently. Pray that your passion for God might be re-ignited and, as you pray, light the candle.

Watch the candle flame flicker and grow. Offer a prayer with thanksgiving to God for the ways he has helped you to shine the light of his love, through your words or actions, wherever you find yourself.

Thank God for the light of his salvation in your life. Leave your candle burning alongside the others and give thanks for your fellow Christians and the light of their faith, which stands alongside yours.

Take a tealight candle away with you and put it somewhere safe at home. When you next feel that your faith is flickering, repeat your prayer, asking again for God's light in your life or in the lives of those known to you.

Wind balloon

Prayer focus: Using a balloon as an illustration, to consider ways in which we can use the strength God gives us, through his Holy Spirit, to share his love with others.

 Bible reflection: *Suddenly a sound like the blowing of a violent wind came from heaven and filled the whole house where they were sitting. They saw what seemed to be tongues of fire that separated and came to rest on each of them. All of them were filled with the Holy Spirit and began to speak in other tongues as the Spirit enabled them.*
ACTS 2:2–4

What I need

- Selection of colourful balloons

- Breath!

- A balloon pump (optional)

Reflect: Reflect on the Holy Spirit as a powerful source of strength, a bit like a tangible wind that is not only powerful but can be life-changing. Consider ways in which the Holy Spirit has strengthened you and encouraged you put your faith into action, as with Jesus' followers at the first Pentecost.

Pray: Select a balloon to blow up. As the balloon inflates, whether with your breath or with air from the balloon pump, begin to pray.

Hold the inflated balloon, pinched closed by your fingers but not tied shut. Pray about how God's Holy Spirit fills you and enlarges your faith and strength.

Say a prayer of thanks for the Holy Spirit at work in your life or ask God for more of his Spirit, if you feel a little 'deflated' spiritually.

Ask God to envision and inspire you, as the early church was inspired at the first Pentecost, and pray that you might know how best to serve the Lord in his strength rather than by your own efforts.

When you are ready, allow the air to seep gently out of the balloon, feeling the moving air on your face. Pray that just as you felt that physical air, so you might feel God's Holy Spirit refreshing your heart and giving you new and deeper strength.

Dove prayer

Prayer focus: To reflect on the peace and comfort that God's Holy Spirit can bring, which scripture describes as being like a dove descending from heaven; to pray for peace.

 Bible reflection: *As soon as Jesus was baptised, he went up out of the water. At that moment heaven was opened, and he saw the Spirit of God descending like a dove and alighting on him.*
MATTHEW 3:16

What I need

- Dove outlines cut from plain white paper or cardboard

- Long length of string or ribbon

- Pegs or sticky tape

- Pens, including felt-tip pens

- Glue sticks and decorative craft items, such as sequins, stickers or ribbons (optional)

Hang the long piece of string or ribbon up, ready for the prayer 'bunting' to be added. Alternatively, if you are in a venue with a suitably low ceiling or available wall, cut shorter lengths of string or ribbon so that each dove can be separately.

Reflect: Consider the gentle nature of God's Holy Spirit as described in scripture. Reflect on the knowledge that God wants you to know peace, not only at Pentecost but always.

Pray: Take a dove outline to decorate as you pray, and take time to sit in peace and comfort while you respond. Write on the dove a prayer or word, or make a drawing, as you feel led. Pray for the calm, still peace that God's Spirit can bring for yourself or others. If available (and if you wish), decorate your dove with craft items.

As you reflect in the stillness and ask for a renewal of peace this Pentecost, give thanks to God for his grace and his Holy Spirit, bringing comfort to those in need.

When you are ready, peg or tape your dove of peace on to the string or ribbon provided. Your dove will help to create a Pentecost bunting decoration. Alternatively, it may hang individually with others to create a flock of doves.

Pentecost prayer for action

Prayer focus: To pray for your community or wider world, that others might know the healing power of God's Holy Spirit and experience his love, which burns like a flame.

 Bible reflection: *'Therefore go and make disciples of all nations, baptising them in the name of the Father and of the Son and of the Holy Spirit, and teaching them to obey everything I have commanded you. And surely I am with you always, to the very end of the age.'*
MATTHEW 28:19–20

What I need

- Large map or photos of your local community, or a drawing or photo of the world or globe

- Red and yellow tissue paper, cut into flame shapes

- Sticky tack or tape

Reflect: At Pentecost, the Holy Spirit was experienced by the early Christians as tongues of fire. Reflect on how we can use this symbol of God's power to encourage us not only to pray but also to go out into our world and share the love of God, empowered by his Holy Spirit.

Pray: Pray for the energy to carry the flame of God's love into your community. As you pray, pick up a tissue paper flame, hold it for a few moments and ask for the chance to share the love of God with others.

When you are ready, tack or tape your tissue paper flame on to the map, photo, drawing or globe as a response to God and a visual sign of your desire to share the fire of his Spirit.

As you create together a map or world that is aflame with the love of God, pray that you will have the energy and opportunities to set your community alight for God.

Take away with you another tissue paper flame as a reminder to carry God's flame of strength and love with you, out into your community and wherever you go.

Chapter 11

Harvest

Bread prayer

Prayer focus: Using the kneading and making of bread, to reflect on and give thanks for God's blessings in our lives; to pray for those who do not have the provisions we have, and also to share our 'harvest' with others.

 Bible reflection: *Our barns will be filled with every kind of provision.*
PSALM 144:13

What I need

- Homemade bread dough, divided into small portions
- Flour
- Baking trays
- Wire cooling trays
- Wipe-clean tablecloth
- An oven
- Greaseproof paper
- Utensils such as forks, cocktail sticks or small rolling pins
- Handwashing facilities

Pre-heat the oven to 220°C/Gas Mark 7.

Reflect: Consider all the blessings you enjoy: plentiful food, warm shelter, love, health, friends, peace, medical care and more. Begin to think also of those who are not so fortunate and who need our prayers and practical support.

Pray: Take a portion of bread dough. On a floured surface, begin to knead and soften it as you bring to God your prayers of thanksgiving for your 'portion' in life.

Shape and mould the dough, perhaps into a round world shape or a heart, or just into a small roll. Decorate with the aid of utensils if you wish. Give thanks for all the things that God provides for you. Begin to pray also for those known to you or in the world as a whole who do not experience such a harvest of blessings and need to know God's love.

Cover a baking tray with greaseproof paper. When you are ready, place your dough on the baking tray and put it in the oven for 8–15 minutes, or until golden brown and cooked through. While the dough is baking, you may want to watch it rise and change, and use this image to pray for change in the world and an end to hunger and suffering.

When it is baked and has cooled down, you may eat your bread and give thanks for the daily provision, the physical and spiritual nourishment, that you receive from God. Alternatively, you may like to give the bread to someone else, sharing with them God's goodness and provision.

Sowing seeds

Prayer focus: To pray for growth, asking God for the strength you need to fulfil the task of sowing seeds of faith; to ask for patience to wait for the harvest that God has for you and those with whom you share your faith.

 Bible reflection: *I waited patiently for the Lord; he turned to me and heard my cry.*
PSALM 40:1

What I need

- Packets of seeds, such as sunflower seeds

- Soil

- Small plant pots

- Watering can filled with tap water

- Plant label sticks and paper

- Marker pen

- Protective table covering

Set up pots with some soil already inside.

Sunflower seeds are good for this prayer activity, as they are easy to handle and only one is needed per pot.

Reflect: God wants to help us to grow in faith, love and knowledge of him and also to share seeds of faith with others, in the hope that they will germinate and grow.

Pray: Take a seed or seeds and pray as you place them in the soil. You may want to ask for growth in your own faith or life, or you might pray, as you plant the seed, that long-held prayers will take root and begin to grow.

Pray for the wisdom and words you need from God to plant seeds of faith in others, through your living faith and actions. Press the seeds firmly into the soil, covering them over and commiting your prayers for growth to God as you do so.

Water the seeds a little, and pray that even when your prayers feel dormant as you await God's work in your life, you will trust that God has a harvest for you.

Use plant label sticks to identify the seeds, for future reference. Take your pot away with you, asking God for patience to wait for the seeds to grow and to care for the plant as it sprouts and grows. Each time you water the plant, pray again for all that God has planted in your life, even if it is not yet visible.

If your seeds do not grow, pray for extra faith in times when prayers seem to go unanswered. Continue to trust that God is at work and that sometimes God's harvest in our life is not the one we imagined.

Loaves and fishes

Prayer focus: To demonstrate that even the smallest offering to God, of our time, gifts or resources, can be used to do immeasurably more than we imagine; to ask for wisdom to know what to give to God and also for trust that he will use it to do big things in his kingdom.

 Bible reflection: *'We have here only five loaves of bread and two fish,' they answered. 'Bring them here to me,' he said. And he told the people to sit down on the grass. Taking the five loaves and the two fish and looking up to heaven, he gave thanks and broke the loaves. Then he gave them to the disciples, and the disciples gave them to the people. They all ate and were satisfied, and the disciples picked up twelve basketfuls of broken pieces that were left over.*
MATTHEW 14:17–20

What I need

- Small loaf shapes cut out of brown or yellow cardboard (or white card, coloured with crayons)
- Small fish shapes cut out of metallic gold or silver cardboard (or white card, coloured with crayons)
- Basket or baskets

Replenish the cardboard loaves and fishes if required.

Reflect: Reflect on the story of the miracle found in Matthew 14. Consider how God can use our 'little' to create a harvest of believers.

Pray: Pray about the gifts you want to give to God for him to use in sharing his love with others, but that you feel are too small. As you name these gifts in prayer, pick up a loaf or fish shape and hold it as you pray.

Let go of any fears you have of not measuring up to others, or any feeling that your resources, time or talents are of no use to God, as you place your small gift into the basket provided.

Know that God can and does use anything we have. We should not underestimate how much God can do with the offering we freely give, however small.

Wheat prayer for the community

Prayer focus: To pray for a planting of God's love in your local community; to ask for God's strength to do all you can to be part of the harvest.

 Bible reflection: *Then he said to his disciples, 'The harvest is plentiful but the workers are few. Ask the Lord of the harvest, therefore, to send out workers into his harvest field.'*

MATTHEW 9:37–38

What I need

• Ears of corn shapes cut from yellow cardboard

• Actual ears of corn (optional)

• Large flipchart page or piece of cardboard

• Sticky tack tape

On the flipchart paper or card, print or draw a large road map of your local community or write a list of places in your community (schools, road names, shopping centres and so on).

Reflect: Consider the steps that you as an individual or a church can take to reap a harvest for God in your community. Look at the places on the map or list in front of you, and reflect on ways you can sow seeds, speak words and act to make a difference for God in your locality.

Pray: Pray for the familiar roads, buildings and places that form your local surroundings. Begin to pray for these places and the people that make up the community where God has currently 'planted' you.

Place an ear of corn on to the map or list, fixing it where you feel most led to do so, as a symbol of your desire to see a great harvest of growth there for God.

Create together a picture of your community filled with a harvest of prayer, and use this image to remind you to pray for your community and to seek God's guidance to be part of his harvest.

Chapter 12

Advent and Christmas

Christmas star prayer

Prayer focus: To consider ways of following God in fresh obedience this Advent and to trust in his promises for your life; to walk the path in which he guides you.

 Bible reflection: *After Jesus was born in Bethlehem in Judea, during the time of King Herod, Magi from the east came to Jerusalem and asked, 'Where is the one who has been born king of the Jews? We saw his star when it rose and have come to worship him.'*
MATTHEW 2:1–2

What I need

- Star shapes cut out of foil or silver cardboard

- Pens

- Sticky tape or pins

- Large piece of dark blue or black cloth

Reflect: Consider ways in which you can follow God this Advent and trust his promises for your life, as the wise men obediently followed the star to Bethlehem.

Pray: Write a prayer on a star as you ask God to make his path for you clear and as you choose to follow him afresh.

When you are ready, attach your star to the cloth, giving your prayers obediently to God and asking him to guide you in his ways.

This response is a symbol of commiting anew to follow God and creates a 'sky' filled with prayer stars.

Holly wreath

Prayer focus: To respond to God by creating a Christmas decoration that reminds us of the sacrifice Jesus made for us all upon the cross; to remember at the same time that Christmas is the beginning of the story.

 Bible reflection: *They put a purple robe on him, then twisted together a crown of thorns and set it on him.*
MARK 15:17

What I need

- Holly leaf shapes cut out of green paper or cardboard

- A circular wreath base cut out of strong plain cardboard

- Glue sticks

- Pens

Reflect: Holly wreaths are often used to decorate homes at Christmas. We can use the holly to represent the crown of thorns worn by Jesus at his crucifixion. As we experience Advent, we can prayerfully think ahead to the sacrifice that the small baby Jesus ultimately made for us.

Pray: Pick up a holly leaf shape and hold it as you begin to pray, perhaps saying a prayer of thanksgiving for the sacrifice that Jesus made or offering yourself, in response, to God's service.

Write a prayer on your leaf and paste it on to the wreath as a sign that you are giving your prayer to God.

Together, the holly leaves will create a decorative wreath of prayers.

Bauble blessings

Prayer focus: To reflect on the gift of salvation and offer prayers of thanksgiving to God; to consider ways of sharing this gift with others.

 Bible reflection: *Their hearts will go out to you, because of the surpassing grace God has given you. Thanks be to God for his indescribable gift!*

2 CORINTHIANS 9:14–15

What I need

- Plain coloured baubles

- Marker pens that will write on the baubles without smudging

- A small undecorated Christmas tree

Reflect: Consider the wonderful gift of salvation with which God has blessed us in Jesus. In the quiet of your heart, reflect on how you might be best able to share this love with others.

Pray: Select a bauble. Write on it a prayer of thanksgiving for the gift of salvation or a prayer asking for a spiritual gift to help you share salvation with others. You may wish to write a word that you want to share with others—for example, 'joy', 'hope' or 'peace'.

Hang your bauble on the tree or take it home to hang on your own tree as a reminder and a symbol of your faith for all to see.

The real gift of Christmas

Prayer focus: To reflect on the meaning of the gift of salvation received at Christmas through Jesus, and how it changes not only our lives but the lives of all who receive it.

 Bible reflection: *Through Christ Jesus the law of the Spirit who gives life has set you free from the law of sin and death.*

ROMANS 8:2

What I need

- Small empty boxes

- Heart shapes cut out of pink paper or card, with 'God's love' or 'Jesus' written on each one

- Christmas giftwrap

- Blank gift tags

- Pens

- Sticky tape

- Gift ribbon (optional)

- A small Christmas tree

Place a heart inside each box, then wrap each box as a gift and add a blank gift tag. Place the gifts under the tree, with pens ready for people to use.

Reflect: Look at the gifts under the Christmas tree. Consider the real gift of salvation, available to us not only at Christmas but all year through because of Jesus.

Pray: Choose a gift from under the tree. Hold it in your hands, looking at it and reflecting on the gift that God gave you in Jesus and all that it means to you. Offer a prayer of thanksgiving and praise to God.

Consider someone in your life with whom you would like to share the gift of Jesus. Write their name on the blank gift tag and pray for them.

Finally, take the gift away with you to give to the person and explain the real gift of God's love. Alternatively, you could place it under your own Christmas tree at home as a commitment to pray for that person.

Section 4

Walking together with God

Chapter 13

Our part in the body of Christ

Handprints

Prayer focus: Using paint handprints, to pray for ways that God can use us as his hands, to do his work in our world; to reflect on the hand of God guiding us in our lives.

 Bible reflection: *For just as each of us has one body with many members, and these members do not all have the same function, so in Christ we, though many, form one body, and each member belongs to all the others. We have different gifts, according to the grace given to each of us.*
ROMANS 12:4–6

What I need

- Coloured paints
- Plastic trays or shallow bowls
- Large piece of paper or individual sheets
- Protective tablecloth
- Handwipes

Reflect: Our handprints are as unique as our blessings and talents, which are all God-given. Consider the talents you have and the ways you can use them to be God's hands in the world.

Pray: Dip your hand in the paint and make a print of your hand on the paper. As you look at your unique print upon the page, begin to pray, perhaps about your abilities, God's hand at work in your life or ways to help others.

Use wipes to clean the paint from your hands, then pick up a a pen. Write a prayer next to your handprint, asking God to use your unique talents for his glory or thanking him for ways that you are being his hands in the world.

Footprints of faith

Prayer focus: Using a physical response, to reflect on our walk with God; to give thanks for the paths he leads us down and his constant presence by our side.

 Bible reflection: *He refreshes my soul. He guides me along the right paths for his name's sake.*
PSALM 23:3

What I need

- Large piece of paper or cardboard (possibly, the reverse of a long length of wrapping paper)

- Coloured pens or felt-tip pens

- Sticky tape

Place the paper or card on the floor and tape or weight it down. Put the coloured pens or felt-tip pens next to it.

Reflect: Think about your walk of faith so far. Reflect on the pathways that God has made clear and the unexpected detours he has walked you through, while never leaving your side.

Pray: Pray about your walk with God and, when you are ready, take a few steps across the paper, drawing around your feet with each step, to depict your unique path of faith. Look back at your footprints and pray about your walk with God. Add a written prayer inside or beside your steps, if you wish.

Finally, ask God to continue to guide your path as you seek to walk as he walked in the world.

Heart for others

Prayer focus: To pray for discernment to glimpse something of God's heart for his world; to pray for those situations that break God's heart and to seek his guidance to take action as part of the body of Christ.

 Bible reflection: *Jesus replied, "'Love the Lord your God with all your heart and with all your soul and with all your mind." This is the first and greatest commandment. And the second is like it: "Love your neighbour as yourself."'*
MATTHEW 22:37–39

What I need

- Large piece of paper or card with a full body outline drawn on it, either fixed on a board or taped on to the floor

- Heart-shaped sticky notes or heart shapes cut out of pink or pale red paper

- Pens or pencils

Reflect: Consider ways in which you can have a heart for others and appreciate afresh the things that break God's heart— the tragic situations and actions that we see around us in his world.

Pray: Take a heart-shaped note or paper and write on it the name of someone or a situation that you long to reach out to. Ask God to place on your heart those places and events that break his heart, and bring them all before him in prayer.

When you are ready, fix your heart shape on to the body outline. Pray that you might know how best to act, pray and support others in need, how to fulfil your particular role in the body of Christ, and how to know more of God's heart.

Through God's eyes

Prayer focus: To seek God's help to look upon the people and circumstances we encounter in the world with his eyes of love and compassion.

 Bible reflection: *I lift up my eyes to the mountains— where does my help come from? My help comes from the Lord, the Maker of heaven and earth.*
PSALM 121:1–2

What I need

- Printed photos (or slideshow of electronic images) showing various crises in the world (for example, war, famine and natural disaster) and contrasting scenes of natural beauty

- Laptop (if displaying images electronically)

Reflect: Reflect on the printed photos or slideshow images of natural beauty and crises situations in our world. Consider the diversity, beauty and devastation depicted. Try to see the images of the world as you think God would see them.

Pray: Pray, as you feel inspired by the images, for God's world and the people who inhabit it. Bring countries and nations before God that are in particular situations of crisis or that are on your heart for any reason. Ask God to open your eyes to those situations that often go unseen but still cause anguish.

When you are ready, leave the station, asking that you may continue to see the world through God's eyes and keep on praying and taking action for change.

Chapter 14

Forgiveness and celebration

Wipe-clean board

Prayer focus: To pray for a fresh start with God—forgiveness, a new beginning and a clean heart.

 Bible reflection: *As far as the east is from the west, so far has he removed our transgressions from us.*
PSALM 103:12

What I need

- Large whiteboard or chalkboard
- Wipe-clean pens or chalk
- Damp cloth

Reflect: Consider any issues, people or situations that come between you and God. Reflect in particular on any personal habits, traits or relationships that hold you back and prevent you from living in freedom.

Pray: When you are ready, write a prayer of confession to God, or a word or picture representing whatever you would like God to erase in your life. It might include such issues as persistent wrong behaviour, unhelpful habits, unforgiveness, past hurts or anger.

Give these issues to God in prayer, confessing and repenting. Affirm your desire to change, and offer up your prayer by using the cloth to wipe away all you have written or drawn.

Know that God does the same whenever we repent or seek to change our hearts or minds. Not a trace of our sin is left, and we can accept a new start. God promises to forgive you and give you a clean slate.

Leave the station, knowing that you are free to live in the grace of forgiveness and that God can help you continue to change.

Washed away

Prayer focus: Using pebbles or sponges, to 'wash away' whatever we know to be damaging our lives and preventing us from walking in freedom with God.

 Bible reflection: *If we confess our sins, he is faithful and just and will forgive us our sins and purify us from all unrighteousness.*
1 JOHN 1:9

What I need

- Pebbles or sponges

- Washable pens

- A bowl of tap water (not too full)

- Waterproof table covering

Check beforehand that the pens will write on the surface of the pebble or sponge and will also wash off again.

Reflect: God promises to wash away our sins and remember them no more. Consider those habits, words, emotions or actions that you would like to confess and give over to God.

Pray: Write words or prayers of repentance on to one of the sponges or pebbles provided, being as honest as you can before God.

Pray for a clean start and the strength to keep turning from wrongdoing as you respond by washing your words away in the bowl of water.

Take your prayer object away with you, now clean of any trace of the words you brought before God. Place it somewhere where it can remind you that God helps us to be transformed and to start afresh.

Torn to shreds

Prayer focus: Using a small document shredder, to 'shred' beyond recognition whatever you want God to remove from your life or help you to overcome.

 Bible reflection: *'Blessed are those whose transgressions are forgiven, whose sins are covered. Blessed is the one whose sin the Lord will never count against them.'*

ROMANS 4:7–8

What I need

- Plain paper

- Pens

- Small document shredder

Reflect: God wants us to give our prayer requests, our hurts and our sins to him and leave them with him. Consider those things you know you need to confess and hand over to God to remove from your life.

Pray: Taking a piece of paper, write a prayer asking for forgiveness or write down the behaviours, actions or habits that you would like to give up with God's help. As you write, pray for God's help and strength.

When you are ready, carefully place the paper into the shredder as a sign that you are giving your prayer to God.

Be assured that God has forgiven you and that you do not need to take the shredded pieces back out of the bin. You can leave the things you wrote with him and walk away.

Celebration of restoration!

Prayer focus: Using Luke 15:7, to celebrate afresh our restoration to God and to remember and rejoice over the time when we first came to faith or a moment when we took a significant step forward in faith.

 Bible reflection: *'I tell you that in the same way there will be more rejoicing in heaven over one sinner who repents than over ninety-nine righteous people who do not need to repent.'*
LUKE 15:7

What I need

- Party food and drink (small cakes, sausage rolls, fizzy pop, crisps and so on)

- Table decorations, such as party hats, crackers or table confetti

- Party poppers

- Disposable party plates, cups and napkins

Lay the table with place settings and food and drink.

Reflect: The Bible says that when someone comes to God and truly repents, there is a celebration in heaven. Recall, if you can, the day you gave your life to God or took a fresh step of commitment, and other special times since then.

Pray: Take your place at the table and help yourself to some food and drink. You can even put on a party hat if you wish: take time to celebrate.

While enjoying the party, give thanks to God in prayer for your salvation and the life he has given you. Know that God and all of heaven rejoice and are celebrating with you. Bring before God in prayer those known to you who have yet to take such a step of faith.

Take a party popper home with you as a reminder to celebrate your faith and to share this joy with others. You may want to pull the party popper at home, at a later date, in another prayer of celebration.

Chapter 15

God's love

Shaping our hearts

Prayer focus: Using modelling clay, to ask God to shape our hearts, refining us into the people he knows we can be, transforming our lives because of his great love for us.

 Bible reflection: *Create in me a pure heart, O God, and renew a steadfast spirit within me.*
PSALM 51:10

What I need

- Modelling dough in various colours (made or bought), separated into smaller pieces

- Plastic board or mat

- Tools, such as rolling pin, plastic cutlery and so on

- Plastic tablecloth

- Small plastic bags (optional)

Reflect: Because of his love for us, God wants to mould or refine our hearts so that we become the loving people he created us to be. Consider ways in which you want God to shape your heart and transform you.

Pray: Take a lump of dough, soften and smooth it in your hands, and bring to God the areas of your heart that need his refining love. Pray about the things that touch your heart—your love, hopes, fears and sorrows. As you pray, mould the dough into a heart shape.

Look at your finished 'heart'. It may still have imperfections and not be fully smoothed, but don't worry. You can remould it until you are happy with it. Pray that God, in the same way, would continue to work on your heart with his refining love.

Take your 'heart' home with you to remind you of God's amazing love and transforming power.

God's love outside the box

Prayer focus: To realise that God's love for us goes beyond all conceivable reason, completely outside the box of our understanding, far greater than we can even imagine.

 Bible reflection: *Give thanks to the Lord, for he is good; his love endures for ever.*
PSALM 106:1

What I need

- A4 paper or cards, with a grid of four squares drawn or printed on each

- Pens or felt-tip pens

Reflect: Look at the empty squares on the page as you think about God's immeasurable love and how it is 'outside the box' of our comprehension.

Pray: Starting in the first box, at the top left, write or draw any ways you already show God's love to others.

In the next box, as a prayer of thanksgiving, write or draw reminders of the ways in which God shows his love for you personally.

As you move into the third box, try to think more widely. Pray about ways in which you could step outside the confines of your comfort zone or 'box' and share God's love with others in a new or different way.

Leave the fourth square blank, to be filled in at another time, when you can reflect again on your other prayer squares. The fourth square should include prayers of thanksgiving and details of ways in which God helped you think and act outside of the box, in his name and with a Christ-like love for others.

Pray through all the boxes before taking your sheet away with you, determined, with God's help, to take steps of faith to love with a love that goes 'outside the box'.

God's love is sweet

Prayer focus: Using heart-shaped biscuits, to reflect on the love of God that can make our life sweet; to ask God for help to share his love with others.

 Bible reflection: *Taste and see that the Lord is good; blessed is the one who takes refuge in him.*
PSALM 34:8

What I need

- Homemade or bought heart-shaped biscuits

- Icing sugar mixed with tap water to make water icing

- Bowls

- Edible decorations (sprinkles, sweets, chocolate buttons and so on)

- Writing icing

Reflect: God's love is a wonderful thing. His words are described in the Bible as being sweeter than honey: 'How sweet are your words to my taste, sweeter than honey to my mouth!' (Psalm 119:103).

Celebrate God's amazing love for you by reflecting on how much he has done for you and how it can sweeten your life, just like the treats set before you.

Pray: Celebrate God's love and the promises in scripture, praying as you add icing to a heart-shaped biscuit. Remember the sweetness of God's love and faithfulness as you add some edible decorations to your biscuit.

You might want to use writing icing to label your biscuit with a word of encouragement, such as 'love' or 'joy', or to write the name of someone with whom you want to share God's love.

Pray as you eat your biscuit, remembering the love of God, or give the biscuit away as a sign of sharing God's love with someone else.

Paper hearts

Prayer focus: To bring to God our hearts—our whole lives, including our weaknesses; to pray for his strength and to draw near to God's heart in obedient trust.

 Bible reflection: *Trust in the Lord with all your heart and lean not on your own understanding.*
PROVERBS 3:5

What I need

- Large heart shape (A4 or larger) cut from dark red cardboard
- Heart shapes cut out of pink or pale red paper, or heart-shaped sticky notes
- Sticky tack
- Small heart-shaped stickers
- Pens

Reflect: God's love is not fragile like paper, but strong and unshakeable. Know and believe that there is nothing you can ever do that would make God love you any less. Reflect on ways in which God has demonstrated his unconditional love and care in your life.

Pray: Take a small paper heart and write on it a prayer of thanks for the ways in which God's love has been evident in your life, or write a prayer for those you love.

Stick the heart on to the large cardboard heart, as a sign that you are giving your 'heart' again to God. Fixing your paper heart firmly to the large heart can also be a symbol of the immensely strong unconditional love of God.

Affirm your prayers by leaving your heart joined to God's 'heart', and taking a small heart sticker from the station. Fix the sticker on to your clothing, or in a place where you will see it regularly, as a reminder to trust in God with all your heart.

Chapter 16

Praying for our community and wider world

Prayer houses

Prayer focus: To create a visual community to inspire prayers for our local community of shops, organisations and people.

 Bible reflection: *Each of us should please our neighbours for their good, to build them up.*
ROMANS 15:2

What I need

- Small house shapes cut from white or pale brown cardboard

- Large sheet of paper or cardboard (flipchart size or bigger)

- Felt-tip pens or marker pens

- Pens for writing

- Sticky tack

Using marker pens, draw an outline of streets on the large sheet of paper, in the correct scale to allow the small house shapes to be stuck on to it. Include other features of the community, such as a park, school, church and so on.

Reflect: We are called by God to shine the light of his grace through our lives and to go out and share his love with others. Look at the outline of streets and other features in front of you and begin to reflect on how you could make a difference for God in your community.

Pray: As you hold a small house shape, pray about your local community. Ask God to help you make your home and your life shine with his love.

You may wish to write a prayer on your house shape or pray for a specific local person or area known to you. Bring the shops, schools, churches and play areas of your locality to God in prayer as you seek to share his love with the inhabitants.

As you continue to pray, stick your house shape on to the outline with sticky tack, to show that it is part of the community. Take some time to look at the picture as a whole and pray for those parts of your community where God's love is needed most, asking God to show you how you can take action.

Community collage

Prayer focus: Using newspaper articles, words and images, to create a collage to aid prayer and reflection; to appreciate afresh the needs of our world and our local community.

 Bible reflection: *Give praise to the Lord, proclaim his name; make known among the nations what he has done.*
PSALM 105:1

What I need

- Newspapers and old magazines

- Paper

- Scissors

- Glue sticks

- Felt-tip pens

Reflect: Newspapers, magazines and broadcast media are full of stories, events and news reports, both positive and negative. Spend some time browsing the reading material provided and reflect on the events and needs of the world. Think also of the good news that is salvation through Jesus.

Pray: Pray as you use the provided materials to create a collage. You may want to include clippings of news stories (both local and international), photos, words and even cartoons.

Bring your community and the wider world before God as you create your prayer collage. Cut out and stick pictures and articles that reflect both the difficult times and the good news to be shared about the world or the community represented.

Spend time in prayer, using the images to remind you of the good news of salvation and the importance of sharing it with others. Give thanks to God and ask his blessing for the world, locally and internationally.

The collage can be displayed as a continual encouragement to prayer and praise, perhaps on a church community focus board.

Paper chain people

Prayer focus: Using paper dolls in a chain, to bring prayers to God for the people in our community.

 Bible reflection: *Therefore I will praise you, Lord, among the nations; I will sing the praises of your name.*
PSALM 18:49

What I need

- Pre-cut strings of paper dolls (or paper and scissors with which to make them)

- Sticky tape

- Pencils

- Felt-tip pens or crayons

- Glue sticks and craft items for decoration (optional)

Reflect: Think about people in your community or known to you personally whom you would like to lift before God in prayer. Also consider the needs of your community as a whole.

Pray: Take a chain of people, and draw features and clothes on to them, praying as you do so. You may wish to add words of prayer for people you know or general prayers for your community as a whole.

When you are finished, you can join your 'community' to the others, using sticky tape, to create a really long chain of people to represent your community.

Display this string of people, all linked together, using it as a reminder to pray for the community around you, asking God to show you what you can do to help others.

Walk of prayer

Prayer focus: To walk, either physically or imaginatively, using visual aids, around the community in which God has placed us; to pray God's love over the streets, homes and broken lives that we may see around us.

 Bible reflection: *Sing the praises of the Lord, enthroned in Zion; proclaim among the nations what he has done.*

PSALM 9:11

What I need

If an actual walk is not possible, display photographs or maps of the local community—its buildings, streets and open spaces—plus leaflets or websites of local businesses, churches or community groups. Website pages can be printed out or displayed on a screen.

Reflect: Think about the community in which you live, with its people, homes, buildings and parks. Begin to reflect on those parts of your community where you feel that God's love is most needed.

Pray: Pray as you walk around your community, either physically or using visual aids, as a group or individually.

Look at your community afresh, trying to see it as God sees it. Which are the areas where prayer or practical help is most needed? Spend time praying for safety, crime prevention, health issues and the spiritual welfare of your local area, as you let the sights and sounds inspire you. Commit the places and people specifically to God's care.

Ask God to help you to walk in the world as Jesus did—to pray, act and seek out the most deprived and troubled areas, which need the transforming touch of God's love.

Pray for the broken places and lives that remain unseen in all communities, asking God to be real in those places and lives.

Section 5

Our personal walk with God

Chapter 17

It's personal

Love letters to God

Prayer focus: To share with God, in letter form, your hopes, fears, thanksgiving and rejoicing.

 Bible reflection: *Do not be anxious about anything, but in every situation, by prayer and petition, with thanksgiving, present your requests to God.*
PHILIPPIANS 4:6

What I need

- Assorted stationery (writing paper or notelets and envelopes)
- Handwriting pens in various colours

Reflect: How often do you text, phone or email a friend or relative? Do you remember to send a card to say 'thank you' or 'I love you'? Do you enjoy receiving letters or emails ? In this age of instant communication it is easy to forget to contact God in prayer. Take time now to write a letter, to communicate to God in the old-fashioned way.

Pray: Write your prayers to God in the style of a letter to a friend or loved one. You might want to say 'thank you', 'sorry' or 'I love you' or just tell God your news, knowing that he delights to hear from you.

When you are done, place your prayer letter in an envelope, but don't seal it. Take it home with you and add more letters over time. You may also find it useful to reread them at a later date, to remind you of answered prayers.

You are a hero

Prayer focus: To give thanks for those people who have made a significant difference in our faith development; to recognise our own ability to be a role model or 'hero' to others.

 Bible reflection: *What you heard from me, keep as the pattern of sound teaching, with faith and love in Christ Jesus.*
2 TIMOTHY 1:13

What I need

- Selection of individually wrapped chocolate treats in a bowl or dish

Reflect: Do you have a hero in your spiritual life—a person who said or did something that made a difference to you? A simple word of encouragement, a sermon or talk or a prayer can all be huge milestones in someone's Christian journey.

You could be someone's hero too (although you may not feel very 'super'). Through something you have said or done, however insignificant it may have felt, you may have planted a seed of faith in someone's heart and changed their life—and that makes you a hero. Do not underestimate what you can do for others and for God.

Pray: Help yourself to some chocolates and, as you enjoy them, pray in some of the following ways.

- Thank God for the 'heroes' in your faith life, naming them before him.

- Pray that you may have the words and skills from God to speak or act so that you can make a difference to others.

- Pray for people you know in every area of your life who may need a 'hero'—a role model to help them know Jesus as their Saviour or to encourage them to grow in their journey of discipleship.

Gospel beads

Prayer focus: To use coloured beads to represent gospel truths; to reflect and pray about them and their importance in our lives.

 Bible reflection: *All are justified freely by his grace through the redemption that came by Christ Jesus.*
ROMANS 3:24

What I need

- Assorted coloured beads (wooden or plastic) in purple, black, red, white or clear, blue and green

- Elastic or cord thread, pre-cut to bracelet lengths, with a knot at one end

- Bowl or tray (or smaller bowls to hold each colour separately)

- Printed cards listing the gospel truths that each colour represents:
  – Purple: majesty of God
  – Black: sin in the world, for which God sent Jesus
  – Red: Jesus' sacrifice, shedding his blood for us
  – White or clear: a clean heart, made new by God
  – Blue: the Holy Spirit, God's gift to us
  – Green: growth in Christ

Reflect: Consider the gospel truths you know—the love and grace that God shows, the sacrifice that Jesus made and the reassurance that can come from knowing him as your Saviour. Spend some time reflecting on these truths and the others listed in the prayer activity.

Pray: Thread each colour of bead on to the length of cord to make either a bracelet or a bookmark. While you thread, read what each colour represents and offer prayers of thanks, share concerns, ask for forgiveness or simply rejoice in these truths.

When you have finished, tie or knot the cord to secure the beads as a completed bracelet or bookmark.

Take your bracelet or bookmark home with you, along with a copy of what the colours represent, for further reflection. You could keep the bookmark in your Bible, diary or current book or wear your bracelet as a reminder.

Fingerprint prayers

Prayer focus: To use our unique fingerprint as an aid to prayer and reflection on the person God made us to be.

 Bible reflection: *'And even the very hairs of your head are all numbered. So don't be afraid; you are worth more than many sparrows. Whoever acknowledges me before others, I will also acknowledge before my Father in heaven.'*
MATTHEW 10:30–32

What I need

- Large cardboard cross
- A quantity of smaller crosses
- Ink pad
- Hand wipes

Reflect: Know that you are made uniquely by God, with your own gifts, struggles, personality and strengths. Just as your fingerprints are unique, there is no other person exactly the same as you. You have a unique role to play in God's purposes.

Pray: Prayerfully consider your gifts, those things that make you unique and special. Give thanks to God for your gifts and ask him to develop you in areas that you feel still need work.

As you pray, press your finger or thumb into the ink pad and make your unique mark on the large cross.

Look at the prints of other people and thank God for our diversity. Also, print your fingerprint on to a smaller cross shape to take away as a reminder that God has purposes for you that are unique to you and your gifts: only you can fulfil those purposes.

Chapter 18

Praying with our senses

Sense of touch

Prayer focus: Using the sense of touch and modelling dough, to pray for God's touch to mould and shape our lives; to give thanks for his presence with us.

 Bible reflection: *May the Lord direct your hearts into God's love and Christ's perseverance.*
2 THESSALONIANS 3:5

What I need

- Coloured modelling dough (homemade or bought), broken into smaller lumps

- Plastic mats or wipe-clean boards

- Tools (rolling pins, plastic cutlery and cocktail sticks)

Reflect: Consider the ways in which God has touched your life, the changes that he has helped you make and the times when you have felt his close presence and experienced his healing touch.

Pray: Take a piece of dough and gently soften it with the warmth of your hands. Thank God for the way he gently shapes and guides us, with care and compassion.

You may wish to choose a colour that represents something to you—for example, green as a symbol of new life or hope.

Shape the dough into anything you want, praying for God to mould you and change you in specific ways. Perhaps give thanks for times in the past when God has held you, healed you or been a very real presence in your circumstances or those of people known to you.

Sense of taste

Prayer focus: To reflect on God's grace and provision in our lives; to acknowledge that he is present both in times that are 'sweet' and in those that are 'sour', and to use our sense of taste to savour our blessings.

 Bible reflection: *How sweet are your words to my taste, sweeter than honey to my mouth!*
PSALM 119:103

What I need

- Various sweets, savoury snacks and sour sweets, in separate bowls

Reflect: Our lives and our Christian walk are filled with moments of joy, difficult times and treasured memories. Reflect on some of these and use the taste of each snack or sweet, and the sensation of eating it, to guide your prayers.

Pray: Enjoy some of the snacks provided, and use the prayer ideas below to guide your thoughts as you eat.

- Sweets: thank God for the good, 'sweet' things he has given you.

- Sour sweets: thank God for helping you through a 'sour' experience, or pray for a current difficult circumstance for you or someone you know.

- Savoury snack: thank God for your treasured moments, times that you want to 'savour'.

Sense of smell

Prayer focus: Using the perfumes and aftershaves provided, to reflect on some memories and praise God for his Spirit, who surrounds us like a sweet perfume.

 Bible reflection: *For we are to God the pleasing aroma of Christ among those who are being saved and those who are perishing.*

2 CORINTHIANS 2:15

What I need

- Bottles of perfume and aftershave (miniatures or small testers are ideal)

Ensure that the lids are secure but easy to open.

Reflect: Different aromas can trigger memories. God is described in the Bible as ever present, like a perfume that surrounds us. Reflect on God's presence in your life and also the ways in which you can be the 'aroma' of Christ (as mentioned in 2 Corinthians 2:15) to those around you.

Pray: Smell the fragrances, giving thanks for fragrant, treasured memories and for God's presence in your everyday life.

If you dislike any of the scents, use them to inspire your prayers about difficulty or unpleasant situations in which you or someone known to you needs to feel God's love and comfort.

Put a little of one of the fragrances you like on your wrist. As you continue through the day, let the scent remind you of God's presence with you always.

Senses of hearing and sight

Prayer focus: To use visual and audio media to inspire our prayers; to appreciate afresh the world God created, and to worship him using images, music and lyrics.

 Bible reflection: *I keep my eyes always on the Lord. With him at my right hand, I will not be shaken.*
PSALM 16:8

What I need

- Images of God's natural world, animals or landscapes, found online or cut out of magazines

- Laptop or board to display images

- CDs or MP3 files of worship music (offering a variety of styles and artists)

- CD player or MP3 player

- Comfortable chairs or beanbags

- Earphones

Set the images out on a table or set up a scrolling slideshow to play continuously on a laptop or other device.

Reflect: Reflect on the wonder of God's creation and the scripture and truths contained in worship songs. You may wish to listen and watch the images, simply spending time resting in God's presence.

Pray: Sit comfortably and allow the images and audio provided to direct your prayers and reflections as you draw near to God.

Look at the images and allow your appreciation and joy in the natural world to form prayers of thanksgiving and awe to your Creator God. You may wish to give thanks for particular aspects of creation or pray for those areas of God's world that are troubled and in some kind of turmoil, whether natural or man-made.

Listen to worship music through the headphones, finding a favourite worship song or discovering a new one. Spend some time quietly praying and worshipping God as you listen to the lyrics.

Chapter 19

You are unique

Your smile

Prayer focus: To give thanks for the joy that God brings to our lives; to reflect on those things that make us unique and give us cause to smile.

 Bible reflection: *Rejoice in the Lord always. I will say it again: rejoice!*
PHILIPPIANS 4:4

What I need

- Pictures of people smiling (different ages, genders and nationalities, and even a few funny animal pictures)

- Smiley face stickers

Reflect: A smile is a unique expression: everyone's smile is different and no one else smiles just like you do. What makes you smile? What do you think makes God smile?

Pray: Look at the pictures provided and rejoice in all that make you personally smile—the blessings God gives you and the people with whom you share happy times. Pray a prayer of thankfulness for these things.

Pray for those people you know who may not be feeling very 'smiley' at the moment (including yourself, if appropriate). Ask God to help you know how you can use your smile to testify to his love in the world.

Take a small smiley face sticker away with you. Stick it somewhere at home as a reminder that, even in difficult times, God is with you and gives you all that makes you unique and wonderful in his sight.

Soap carving

Prayer focus: To know that you are a true masterpiece in the eyes of God, your Creator; to reflect and pray about ways you feel you need refining and to seek the acceptance that only God can provide.

 Bible reflection: *Bring… everyone who is called by my name, whom I created for my glory, whom I formed and made.*

ISAIAH 43:6–7

What I need

- Pieces of soap (either large bars divided into chunks or smaller individual bars)

- Tools for carving, such as plastic knives

- Plastic mats or boards

Reflect: Sometimes it takes a lot of work to make something from scratch: think about a wood carver painstakingly working to make something beautiful, or an artist creating a painting on a blank canvas. God sometimes needs to chip away a lot of unnecessary things in our lives as he makes us into the perfect masterpiece he knows we have potential to be, because he created us.

Pray: Carve away some of the soap to create something new. It doesn't have to be perfect or beautiful or resemble anything in particular. You are just changing it, with each piece that you carve away.

Pray as you carve into the soap and see bits fall off. Give to God those areas of your life that you feel need work: ask God to 'chip away' at them and allow him to reveal in you the masterpiece he created you to be.

Mirror, mirror!

Prayer focus: To use our own reflection to pray for God's perspective on ourselves; to acknowledge our worth in God's eyes, however much we lack self-confidence.

 Bible reflection: *For we are God's handiwork, created in Christ Jesus to do good works, which God prepared in advance for us to do.*
EPHESIANS 2:10

What I need

- A mirror

- Open Bibles or printed copies of Ephesians 2:10

Reflect: Everyone has times when they don't like to look in a mirror because they feel critical of their own appearance. Read Ephesians 2:10 and know that you are God's handiwork, created for a purpose, and that he loves you just the way you are.

Pray: Look at your face in the mirror for a few moments. Consider your favourite features and resist any feelings of self-criticism. God made you just as you are and wants you to know that you are beautiful in his sight.

The world judges by appearance and sets unrealistic expectations on us all to conform to certain standards of 'beauty'. Give thanks that God made you, and understand that you are truly loved and entirely perfect in the eyes of your Creator.

Pray for the confidence that can only come from knowing God. He wants you to feel worthy and secure in your unique abilities and personality.

Tactile objects

Prayer focus: To use tactile objects to inspire prayers, aid focus and enable you to engage with God.

 Bible reflection: *I call on you, my God, for you will answer me; turn your ear to me and hear my prayer.*
PSALM 17:6

What I need

- Tactile objects—for example, a prayer cross, fish shape, wooden or ceramic heart, and pebbles inscribed with words like 'hope', 'peace' and grace', bought or sourced from a beach or riverbed.

- Decorative mat or cloth

Reflect: It is sometimes difficult to concentrate on praying because so many external and internal distractions crowd into our minds. Often we feel we don't know what to say or don't have the ability to put our prayers into words. Having something to focus on, an object to hold, can really help.

Pray: Select an object from those provided and, when you feel ready, hold it in your hand, using its shape, texture and whatever meaning it has for you to guide you in your prayers. You may wish to give thanks for the ways in which God has 'smoothed' an area of your life or personality, or for his faithfulness and the hope he provides when we call on him.

You may want to offer a prayer of repentance or simply rest in God's presence with your eyes closed, allowing him to speak to you in some way.

Take your time in prayer, focusing on what the items symbolise to you. Use as many of the objects, one by one, as you wish.

When you are ready, place them back down as a response to God, giving all that you have been reflecting on into his hands.

Chapter 20

The Potter's hand

Clay pots

Prayer focus: Using a malleable clay medium, to pray creatively to the God who moulded and formed us and who continues to transform us into his likeness.

 Bible reflection: *But we have this treasure in jars of clay to show that this all-surpassing power is from God and not from us.*

2 CORINTHIANS 4:7

What I need

• Homemade brown modelling dough or bought clay, separated into smaller lumps

• Tools (rolling pins, plastic cutlery and so on)

• Wipe-clean boards

• Handwipes

Reflect: Take a piece of clay and begin to soften and mould it in your hand. Reflect on the ways that God has moulded your life and character or the ways in which you feel you still need moulding.

Pray: When you are ready, take the softened modelling material and shape it into a small pot while you continue to pray.

Your creation may not be perfect but it can be reshaped a few times as you pray. Use the forming of your clay pot and its imperfections to remind you that God is still at work, moulding you into what he desires you to be.

Take your pot away with you as a reminder of God the potter, who wants you to continue seeking his touch to shape and refine you.

Paper pots

Prayer focus: To consider the biblical metaphor of God as a potter who moulds and perfects us, his dearly loved creations, and to write prayers of thanksgiving to him.

 Bible reflection: *Yet you, Lord, are our Father. We are the clay, you are the potter; we are all the work of your hand.*
ISAIAH 64:8

What I need

- Outlines of clay pots drawn or printed on small squares of paper (four to a sheet of A4, cut into individual sheets)

- Pens

- Scissors

Reflect: God created you from scratch, designing you to be exactly the person he intended you to be. Reflect on God the Creator, who formed your very being as a potter moulds clay.

Pray: Write a prayer on the picture of a pot—perhaps a prayer of thanks to God for the individual qualities with which he has blessed you, for his creative power and for your life itself.

Consider ways in which knowing God has shaped your life. Pray with thankfulness and ask for his Spirit to mould you in further ways.

You can cut around your pot or leave it on the page. Finish in prayer by placing your life and all that you are into the 'potter's hands' once again.

Tile smash and mosaic

Prayer focus: To bring to God in prayer those things that hinder us from being all that he intends us to be; to 'smash' the things that hold us back, asking God to be at work in our lives to shape us.

 Bible reflection: *'Can I not do with you, Israel, as this potter does?' declares the Lord. 'Like clay in the hand of the potter, so are you in my hand, Israel.'*
JEREMIAH 18:6

What I need

- Coloured ceramic tiles (or white tiles painted in bright colours)
- A small hammer
- Marker pens that will write on the back of ceramic tiles
- Large board, cut into the shape of a jar or other appropriate shape
- Strong glue and spatula

Make sure there is a safe surface for the tile smash. You may want to set up the station outdoors.

Reflect: What things—physical, emotional or spiritual—do you need to 'break' and let go of, to allow God to mould you?

Pray: Choose a ceramic tile and write words or a prayer on its reverse with a marker pen. You may want to include anything you want God to 'break' in your life—hurts, fear, anger, pride, jealousy, negative attitudes and so on.

Pray these words or prayer and, as you do so, take the hammer and smash the tile into small pieces. Pray that God would smash these obstructions to your walk with him.

Working as a group, take the broken pieces, which appear useless, and glue them on to the board to form a mosaic. As you do this, pray that God will create beauty from brokenness, using the broken pieces in your life.

When the activity is finished, the mosaic can be grouted and displayed as a reminder of how God can form us into a new creation.

Broken jars of clay

Prayer focus: Using pieces of broken clay pot, to reflect on God's power to break the things that bind us, and then to restore us and make us stronger.

 Bible reflection: *But the pot he was shaping from the clay was marred in his hands; so the potter formed it into another pot, shaping it as seemed best to him.*
JEREMIAH 18:4

What I need

- Small pieces of broken clay or terracotta (a flowerpot is ideal)
- A large ceramic vase or jar

Reflect: God can use even the most 'broken' vessel to share his love, and it is often when we feel at our most broken that God can reveal his strength. Consider when God has been your strength, perhaps in times of weakness or ill health, and has restored you.

Pray: Take a piece of broken clay and look at it. As you reflect on its broken appearance, pray about the jagged 'edges' that you feel existing in you. Bring to God in prayer any such brokenness that you feel.

When you are ready, place the broken piece of clay into the larger jar, to signify that you are trusting your life and brokenness into God's hands.

Believe that, however you feel now, God can bring restoration and can use times of difficulty to build you into a stronger person, made more perfect by your weakness and your reliance on his strength.

Appendix

Prayer spinner
template

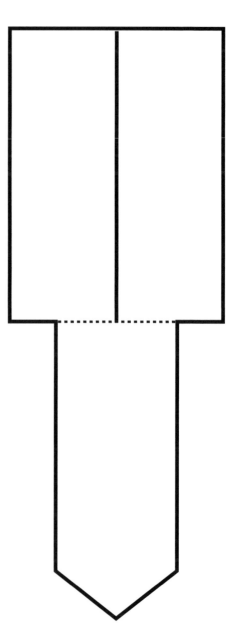

Reproduced with permission from *80 Creative Prayer Ideas* by Claire Daniel (BRF, 2014) www.brfonline.org.uk

Prayer pinwheel template

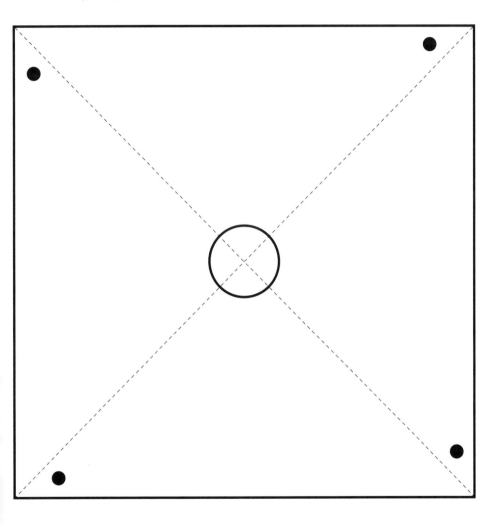

Cut along dotted lines to the centre circle, hole punch corners
and cut a hole where the dotted lines cross in the centre.

Reproduced with permission from *80 Creative Prayer Ideas* by Claire Daniel (BRF, 2014) www.brfonline.org.uk

Bible passage index

Old Testament

New Testament

Prayer topic index